D1089712

CHRISTIAN MYSTICS

WAYS OF THE CHRISTIAN MYSTICS

THOMAS MERTON

SHAMBHALA
Boston
1994

Shambhala Publications, Inc.
Horticultural Hall
300 Massachusetts Avenue
Boston, Massachusetts 02115

© 1961, 1962, 1964, 1965, 1966, 1967
by the Abbey of Gethsemani.
Copyright renewed 1989, 1990, 1992, 1993.
Published by arrangement with Farrar,
Straus & Giroux, Inc.

9 8 7 6 5 4 3 2 1

First Shambhala Edition
Printed in Singapore on acid-free paper ∞
Distributed in the United States by Random House, Inc.,
and in Canada by Random House of Canada Ltd

See page 219 for Library of Congress
Cataloging-in-Publication data.
See page 217 for imprimatur.

CONTENTS

WAYS OF THE
CHRISTIAN MYSTICS

FROM PILGRIMAGE
TO CRUSADE

THE "SACRED JOURNEY" has origins
in prehistoric religious cultures and
myths. Man instinctively regards himself as
a wanderer and wayfarer, and it is second
nature for him to go on pilgrimage in
search of a privileged and holy place, a
center and source of indefectible life. This
hope is built into his psychology, and
whether he acts it out or simply dreams
it, his heart seeks to return to a mythical
source, a place of "origin," the "home"
where the ancestors came from, the
mountain where the ancient fathers were
in direct communication with heaven, the
place of the creation of the world, paradise
itself, with its sacred tree of life.[1]

In the traditions of all the great religions, pilgrimage takes the faithful back to the source and center of the religion itself, the place of theophany, of cleansing, renewal, and salvation. For the Christian there is, of course, Jerusalem, the Holy Sepulchre, where the definitive victory of life over death, good over evil, was won. And there is Rome, the center of the Catholic Church, the See of Peter, the place of indulgence and forgiveness. There are also grottoes and springs blessed by visitations of the merciful Mother, sites of repentance and of healing. There are countless tombs of saints, places of hierophany and of joy.

Christian pilgrimages to Jerusalem, which simply followed the example and pattern of much older Jewish pilgrimages, began in the fourth century A.D. St. Helena's pilgrimage and the finding of the True Cross took place in 326. Less than ten

years later, the splendid Basilica of the
Holy Sepulchre was dedicated. It would
attract thousands of pilgrims from the
West. Already, in 333, a pilgrim from Bor-
deaux, in France, was writing about his
visit to the Holy Places. One of the liveli-
est and most interesting of all written pilgrimages is that of the nun Aetheria,[2] who
probably came from Spain and visited not
only the Holy Places in Jerusalem but the
monks of the Egyptian desert and of Palestine, even going through the Arabian desert to Mount Sinai, where there was as
yet no monastery, but where there were
colonies of hermits living in huts and
caves. Large numbers of these anchorites
escorted her enthusiastically to the sum-
mit of the mountain, where appropriate
texts from the Bible were read, Mass was
sung, *eulogiae* or spiritual gifts (consisting
of fruits from the monks' orchard) were
passed around, and the joys of the Chris-

tian life were generally celebrated in the very place where God had given the Law to Moses. Note that at this same time St. Gregory of Nyssa was writing his life of Moses,[3] which is in fact a description of the mystical itinerary and ascent of the monk to God in "dark contemplation." The geographical pilgrimage is the symbolic acting out of an inner journey. The inner journey is the interpolation of the meanings and signs of the outer pilgrimage. One can have one without the other. It is best to have both. History would show the fatality and doom that would attend on the external pilgrimage with no interior spiritual integration, a divisive and disintegrated wandering, without understanding and without the fulfillment of any humble inner quest. In such pilgrimage no blessing is found within, and so the outward journey is cursed with alienation. Historically, we find a progressive "interiorization" of the pilgrimage theme, until in monastic literature the "peregrinatio" of the monk is entirely spiritual and is in fact synonymous with monastic stability.[4]

Aetheria's account of her pilgrimage tells us much about the liturgy of fourth-century Jerusalem, where the Holy Sepulchre was regarded as the normal station for daily celebration of the Eucharist, and where the True Cross was set up under the roof of the same basilica, on what remained of the rock of Calvary (Aetheria calls it simply the *martyrium* — the place of martyrdom or of witness). Note that even though Calvary was there, the Eucharist was celebrated specifically at the Holy Sepulchre, not on Calvary. The sacred events of the New Testament were reenacted liturgically at the place where they actually happened. The liturgy of other places in the Christian world was simply intended to reproduce and remind the pilgrim of what he could see in its perfection at Jerusalem. Jerusalem was in every sense the "center of the world," not only in terms of ancient geography, but in the more important and sacred sense. It was the center par excellence of *Truth,* the place of the *True* Cross, of which all other crosses would be mementos and representations; the place of the true Holy Sepulchre, which would be recalled by the sepulchres of the martyrs in each altar of sacrifice: the place where the Saviour had truly walked, spoken, preached, healed, suffered, risen, ascended. The places themselves in their reality bore witness to that truth: but they were, far more than that, sacraments of truth and of a special life-giving presence.[5] If Jerusalem was the place of the *anastasis,* the resurrection, the regions around it were filled with the *martyria,* where the apostles and saints had borne witness to the power of the resurrection. Finally, there were the monks in all the deserts of Syria, Palestine, Arabia, and Egypt who were living witnesses of the resurrection. The pilgrimage of Aetheria was, then, a sacred journey to the center from which the whole Christian world was charged with the true presence of the resurrection and glory of the Saviour.

II

The fall of Rome to the Barbarians in the beginning of the sixth century and the invasions that poured down over the East as well as over Western Europe temporarily cut off the Holy Land from the West. Though Jerusalem was then practically inaccessible to most European Christians, pilgrimages continued unabated elsewhere. But now they received a new character, imprinted upon them by the Celtic monks of Ireland.

Peregrinatio, or "going forth into strange countries," was a characteristically Irish form of asceticism. The Irish *peregrinus*, or pilgrim, set out on his journey, not in order to visit a sacred shrine, but in search of solitude and exile. His pilgrimage was an exercise in ascetic homelessness and wandering.[6] He entrusted himself to Providence, setting out with no definite aim, abandoning himself to the Lord of the universe. Since Ireland is an island, this meant entrusting oneself to the hazards of sea travel, and there are records of Irish *peregrini* who simply floated off aimlessly into the sea, abandoning themselves to wind and current, in the hope of being led to the place of solitude which God Himself would pick for them. In this way, some came to Wales or Cornwall or to the isles of western Scotland. Others, doubtless the majority, made use of their considerable skill in navigation and followed indications that had perhaps come to them down years of seafaring tradition. Such were St. Columba, founder of the great monastic center at Iona,[7] and St. Brendan, whose legendary voyages[8] are thought, by some, to have brought him even to America. This has still to be convincingly proved. But there is historical evidence that Irish monks were in Iceland[9] before the coming of the Danes in the eighth century, and they had also visited the Faroe Islands, as well as the Shetlands and the Orkneys, not to mention Brittany, which was entirely populated by Welsh and Irish colonists, mostly monks, in the sixth century.

It is true, of course, that many of these pilgrimages brought Irish monks into in-habited places where the natives were willing and ready to receive the Christian message. The monks then became mission-aries. The main reason for their journeys was not the missionary apostolate but the desire of voluntary exile.[10]

An *Old Irish Life of St. Columba* (a pane-gyric, not to be confused with the essen-tially historical life by Adomnan) describes the pilgrim spirit as belonging to the very essence of Christianity:

> God counselled Abraham to leave his own country and go in pilgrimage into the land which God had shown him, to wit the "Land of Promise." . . . Now the good counsel which God enjoined here on the father of the faithful is incumbent on all the faithful; that is to leave their country and their land, their wealth and their worldly delight for the sake of the Lord of the Elements, and go in perfect pilgrimage in imitation of him.[11]

The example of Abraham inspired many other Irish pilgrims, including Saint

Cadroe, and his companions, who went forth to seek the land which the Lord "would show them."[12]

It was, of course, the vision of the "Land Promised to the Saints" that inspired the fabulous voyage of Brendan and his monks. In Celtic pilgrimages there is a reawakening of the archaic mythical theme of the "return to paradise"[13] under the guidance of God or of His angels. But this is something more than "mere myth." The mystic spirituality of the Celtic monks is built on a charism of pilgrimage and navigation.

The objective of the monk's pilgrimage on earth may be imaginatively described as the quest of the "promised land" and "paradise," but more theologically this goal was described as the "place of resurrection"[14]—the place divinely appointed, in which the monk is to settle down, spend the rest of his days in solitude, doing penance, praying, waiting for the day of his death. To leave Ireland in search of this privileged place was to "go on pilgrimage for the love of God" (*peregrinari pro Dei amore*) or "in the name of God." If the pilgrimage were a "navigation," then the monk was seeking for a "desert in the sea."[15] The Irish had a predilection for lonely islands.[16] In the voyage of St. Brendan, one of the Faroe Islands covered with wild sea birds becomes transformed into a monastic and liturgical paradise, the place par excellence for the celebration of the Easter mystery.[17] The Holy Sepulchre has been replaced by the Desert Island. In any event, the object of pilgrimage is to take the monk to his peculiar and appointed place on the face of the earth, a place not determined by nature, race, and society, but by the free choice of God. Here he was to live, praise God, and finally die. His body would then be buried in this spot, and would there await the resurrection. The pilgrimage of the Celtic monk was not then just endless and aimless wandering for its own sake. It was a journey to a mysterious, unknown, but divinely appointed place, which was to be the place of the monk's ultimate meeting with God.

In the eighth and ninth centuries, when communication with the East was once again open, Irish monks went on pilgrimages to Egypt and the Holy Land, and in many cases their desire was either to settle at a Holy Place and die there, or else to find "the place of their resurrection" on the way back, and remain there, often as recluses, or solitaries living in completely enclosed cells built against the wall of a Church.[18] Thus, the ninth and tenth centuries record the presence of scores of Irish monks living in cities of Germany, Burgundy, Lorraine, etc., either as scholars teaching in schools or as recluses.[19]

Soon there were many secondary aims in the pilgrimage. Monks went to spend a time in *peregrinatio* with other monks and in monastic centers where they could find instruction and example. Or else they went to obtain liturgical and other books,[20] which they copied in their own monasteries. The five pilgrimages of St. Benedict Biscop to Rome are famous examples of this. Others went to Rome to obtain relics needed in the dedication of monastic churches or altars.[21] Some even went on pilgrimages in the hope of martyrdom;[22] others to escape death at the hands of invading Vikings.

Whatever one may think about some of the special forms taken by the Celtic *peregrinatio,* the records, historical as well as literary, bear witness to a profound spiritual integration in the culture from which this practice emerged. The external and geographic pilgrimage was evidently, in most cases, something more than the acting out of psychic obsessions and instabilities. It was in profound relationship with an inner experience of *continuity* between the natural and the supernatural, between the sacred and the profane, between this world and the next: a continuity both in time and in space.[23] For the Celt, as for archaic and primitive man, the true reality is that which is manifested obscurely and sacramentally in symbol, sacrament, and myth. The deepest and most mysterious potentialities of the physical and bodily world, potentialities essentially sacred, demanded to be worked out on a spiritual and human level.

The pilgrimage of the Irish monk was therefore not merely the restless search of an unsatisfied romantic heart. It was a profound and existential tribute to realities perceived in the very structure of the world, and of man, and of their being: a sense of ontological and spiritual dialogue between man and creation in which spiritual and bodily realities interweave and interlace themselves like manuscript illuminations in the Book of Kells. This resulted in an astounding spiritual creativity which made it impossible for the Celtic monk merely to accept his existence as something static and "given," or his monastic vocation as a juridically stabilized and sedentary existence. His vocation was to mystery and growth, to liberty and abandonment to God, in self-commitment to the apparent irrationality of the winds and the seas, in witness to the wisdom of God the Father and Lord of the elements. Better perhaps than the Greeks, some of the Celtic monks arrived at the purity of that *theoria physike* which sees God not in the essences or *logoi* of things, but in a hierophanic cosmos; hence the marvelous vernacular nature poetry of the sixth and seventh century Celtic hermits.[24]

As Dom Jean Leclercq points out,[25] pilgrimage was to remain a "form of hermit life" and a logical though exceptional, constituent of the monastic vocation.

III

In the meantime, quite a different concept of "pilgrimage" was growing up in Irish circles.

The penitential systems of Ireland and Anglo-Saxon England in the sixth to the tenth centuries completely transformed the old concept of ecclesiastical penance.[26] In primitive Christianity, the only formal penance imposed by the Church was public penance, and in the earliest times this could be performed only once. The transition to private and indefinitely repeatable penance was made under Celtic influence.

One of the most important forms of penance was *peregrinatio,* pilgrimage, or exile, especially to an island, *relegatio in insulam.*[27] Instead of doing public penance in full view of the local church (for instance, by remaining outside the church in penitential garb, fasting and performing other prescribed works until reconciled), the penitent was sent off into exile, either perpetual or temporary. He might be sent to a lonely island, or simply turned out into the alien world to wander without a specified goal. The penitent just "peregrinated." Only after the eighth century is the penitent sent to a specific place, or perhaps to a distant bishop to *receive* a penance, and then when he returned to his own church, after giving proof that his penance was completed, he was absolved. We must always remember that at this time absolution was given only after the penance had been completed. After the ninth century, the goal of the penitent pilgrim was most often Rome, where he was sent to have the Pope decide his case and impose a suitable penance and send him back to his own bishop for absolution. Some penitents preferred to go direct to Rome, over the head of their own bishop, but this was reproved.[28]

It is not quite exact to regard this *peregrinatio* as a purely private and face-saving form of penance. On the contrary, it had a semi-public character[29] and was imposed for scandalous faults. The penitent pilgrim was driven forth as an outcast, dressed in rags or sackcloth, barefoot, perhaps even wearing a chain.[30] He was under strict obligation to keep moving, for he was a "wanderer" ("Let him not spend the night twice in the same place," said one of the Penitentials).[31] He was not allowed to bear arms, and was therefore sent totally defenseless among strangers who might be barbarians and pagans (for instance, the Picts in Scotland or many of the inhabitants of lands east of the Rhine). The pilgrim who was carrying out a canonical penance wore a distinctive garb and badge. The pilgrim thus became a familiar figure in the Europe of the Dark Ages, and he was easily recognizable as a sacred person. If he were a canonical penitent, he was, like Cain, one on whom the curse of God rested, one who was being punished and healed, whom *man might not touch* (Gen. 4:13–15). He was, so to speak, a holy outcast, a consecrated tramp, living under a mystery of execration and protection, overshadowed by inscrutable love, a mystery and portent to every man. It was a sacred duty to protect him, feed him, give him shelter, and show him his way. Failure to shelter and protect pilgrims was declared to be the reason for punishment by an invasion of Lombards in southern

France.[32] Since one could not count even on the faithful to respect the pilgrim and penitent, these travelers were sometimes provided with official letters of identification.[33] Special hostelries for the numerous Irish and Anglo-Saxon pilgrims were provided both at the chief places of pilgrimage and on the way there, and the Anglo-Saxon hostelry in Rome was supported by taxation in England.[34] Thus the penitent pilgrim, though cast out, had a very definite and indeed privileged place in the Church.

Pilgrimage or perpetual exile was usually given as penances for the worst crimes:[35] murder, incest, sacrilegious sins of violence or lust; and if the penitent was convinced of his need for penance and forgiveness, there is no question that he would take his penance seriously. Unfortunately, when it became common to send the worst offenders on pilgrimage as penance for grave crimes, large numbers of criminals were in effect turned loose, to live an irresponsible and wandering existence in common.[36] They naturally tended to band together, and when they did, their influence on each other was perhaps not much help in carrying forward their repentance and conversion.

Alcuin complained, in a letter,[37] of the dangers that came from associating with the riffraff of the roads, the jugglers, the thieves, and the pilgrims of various shades and dispositions who were met everywhere. Even genuine pilgrims who fell in with these others tended to suffer grave damage from their contact, and St. Boniface lamented that there was hardly a city on the way from England to Rome that did not have a few fallen Anglo-Saxon women living there as whores.[38] They were among the many for whom pilgrimage, on the Continent, was hardly a spiritual success.

Note that on the Continent especially, pilgrimage was imposed as penance on clerics and monks who were considered scandalous and even incorrigible, doubtless as a last resort.[39] In fact, since the monk was already living in a public state of penance, he was not able to perform the ordinary public penance according to the ancient and solemn discipline. The paradoxical result of the penitential pilgrimage in the Middle Ages was to *increase* scandal by turning loose clerics and monks of disordered life to wander in public in situations that invited them to further sins that could hardly be kept hidden.[40] There was consequently a strong reaction on the part of the eleventh-century reformers against the "gyrovagues" or wandering monks.[41]

We have seen that pilgrimages were originally intended as expiation, by a defenseless and nonviolent, wandering existence, of the worst crimes of violence.

Now in the ninth and tenth centuries, even killing in war was regarded as a sin requiring expiation.[42] In the Anglo-Saxon penitential of Theodore of Canterbury, a soldier who killed a man in war was obliged to a forty-day fast even though he might have killed his enemy in the "ordinary line of duty," under obedience to his officer. Later penitentials distinguished between offensive and defensive killing. One who attacked an enemy and killed him was obliged to do penance. One who killed another in self-defense was not obliged to do penance, but was *counseled* to do so for the good of his soul. Burchard of Worms, in the eleventh century, equated killing in war with ordinary homicide and assigned seven years of penance, without distinction as to offense or defense.[43]

Pilgrimage was not usually given as a penance for killing in war. But persons who had accumulated many penances for various sins might find themselves faced with a staggering burden of penitential "tariffs" to pay off. In order not to have to fast and do penance for scores of years, they had their multiple penance commuted to a single pilgrimage, which took care of everything.

With this, the systematization of pilgrimage began, and pilgrimages were imposed by the Inquisition as afflictive punishments.[44] The Church recognized places of major pilgrimage, such as Jerusalem and Rome, Canterbury and Compostela. There were also minor places of pilgrimage such as Le Puy, St. Gilles, Rocamadour, in France.[45] Ponce de Léras, a twelfth-century brigand in the central mountains of France, abandoned his life of brigandage, made restitution, went on pilgrimage to Compostela, and returned to settle down in a Cistercian monastery he had founded.[46] This was a standard medieval pattern for a successful conversion of life. As a matter of fact, it introduces us to a new pattern, in which "wandering eremitism" is no longer favored as an ascetic ideal, and in which the *peregrinatio* of Abraham is imitated by the monk who leaves "the world" for the cloister and stability of the monastery. In the eleventh and twelfth centuries we find frequent attacks upon "false hermits" who wander about. The monk who has entered the cloister will no longer leave to wander further afield. His perfection will consist in his stability.[47] However, as Dom Leclercq points out,[48] the monk in the cloister will read the narratives of saintly pilgrims as his "adventure stories." He will also take a passionate interest in the Crusades. As a matter of fact, in the case of the Crusades, an exception will be made. Many Cistercians accompanied the Crusades as chaplains, and Cistercian foundations were made in the Near East. In any case, the same spiritual crisis which led to monastic reforms in the eleventh and twelfth centuries led at the same time to a revival of itinerant eremitism and also, above all, to the great mass-*peregrinatio* of the Crusade.[49]

IV

It is often thought that the sole or chief reason for the Crusades was the fact that Christian pilgrims suffered harassment from the Moslems who were masters of Jerusalem.[50] It is certain that the popular enthusiasm that drove thousands of knights and common soldiers to the East in 1095 was an eruption of zeal for the liberation of the Holy Sepulchre. But it must be remembered that the first idea of the Crusade, which goes back to Gregory VII in 1074, was a project for the defense of Constantinople, an essentially "ecumenical" venture, by which it was hoped that the union of Greek and Latin against the Turk would heal the schism that had begun in 1054. Actually Constantinople was a holy city and a place of pilgrimage. The First Crusade was itself an enormous pilgrimage, a holy war preached and organized by the Church, led by an armed bishop, Adhemar, ordinary of Le Puy, one of the "minor" places of pilgrimage in France. The various armies converged on Constantinople, and then went on to take Jerusalem.

Pilgrimages to Jerusalem had opened a familiar way to the armies of the Cross. In the first half of the eleventh century, Robert II, Duke of Normandy, had to make a barefoot pilgrimage to Jerusalem to expiate the murder of his brother, Duke Richard III.[51] In 1073, Count Theodore, murderer of Conrad, Archbishop of Trier, went to Jerusalem. These two examples among many[52] show that the Crusaders were not all launching out into the unknown. Noblemen who had done penance and visited the Holy Sepulchre were now also attracted by the prospect of settling in this most sacred of lands, and having castles of their own in Judea or Galilee, there to await the second coming of Christ and the resurrection.

In the mind of Pope Urban II, the Holy Crusade was to be not only a great unification of Christendom against the Turk, but a magnificent and general act of repentant faith that would culminate in the moral reform and total renewal of Christendom. The "land of promise" which the Holy Father envisioned was a general state of holiness, unity, and perfection in the whole Church, East and West, a Christendom united and renewed in peace at the Holy Sepulchre.

Since the ninth century, very serious and sustained efforts had been made to limit wars among Christians. While promulgating the Crusade, the Council of Clermont (1095) also made the "Truce of God" of general obligation. This prohibition of fighting, from Septuagesima to Trinity Sunday and from Wednesday to Monday all year, had previously been imposed by local councils. Pope Urban was seeking a paradise of peace in Christendom, united in defense of the Holy Land, which symbolized the peace promised to all men of good will. As a Catholic historian observes,[53] "he commanded Christians to make a truce to all hostility that sprang from private interests. Thus the very notion of war was altered under the influence of the Roman Pontiff." War was now to be waged only in obedience to the Church, which was intent upon restricting the use of violence to what was absolutely necessary for the defense of Christendom. In the sense that the Crusade was expected to unify Christendom and consolidate Christian power in a way that would permanently subdue Islam and hold off all future aggression from without, it was explicitly considered a "war to end wars." This eschatological hope accounted in part for the tremendous expectation and enthusiasm of the first Crusaders.[54] War against the infidel now became a sacred duty for all because it was the pledge of unity and peace within Christendom as well as of permanent peace for the Christian world. Hence, the Crusade was considered one of the greatest and most meritorious good works. There was no "Truce of God" in killing Turks, because the sooner the great work was accomplished, the better it would be for all.

But above all, in the intentions of the Popes, the Crusade remained essentially a pilgrimage, but a mass pilgrimage of all Christians united in the expectation of the imminent return of Christ. The eschatological hope was expressed in the hymns and marching songs of the Crusaders.[55] Just as pilgrimage had been the commutation of all other penances, so now the Crusade, the super-pilgrimage, amply satisfied for the sins of a whole lifetime, even a lifetime of brigandage, lechery, murder, blasphemy, impiety, anything. The Crusade became the *epitome of all penance.* In fact, there was a great deal of penitential ardor among the first Crusaders. They fasted and prayed before battles and multiplied processions and acts of devotion. They were in general dedicated to a true spirit of poverty and austerity befitting pilgrims. The proof of one's profound and sincere conversion and loyalty to Christ and His Church was one's readiness to undergo hardship and privation, and do battle against an enemy who, quite naturally, came to be regarded as the incarnation of all the forces of evil. St. Bernard emphasized that the presence of infidels at the Holy Sepulchre was an outrage and insult to the Saviour.[56] Urban II at Clermont urged the faithful to take up arms against an "abominable . . . impure people . . . [who had] ravaged and stained the holy places."[57] He had barely uttered his call when the cry went up everywhere: *Deus vult!* "God wills it!" The same cry, "It is written!," had launched the Moslems, a people of pilgrimage, upon the holy war.

It has been noted about St. Bernard (who preached the Second Crusade) that a deep vein of Augustinian pessimism about fallen man in a world of sin colored his ideas.[58] For St. Bernard, salvation outside a monastery was, to say the least, extremely difficult and doubtful. Though he was himself not friendly to pilgrimages for monks, he felt that the Crusade offered a unique opportunity for penance and salvation for multitudes of Christians who would otherwise most certainly be damned. "I call blessed the generation that can seize an opportunity of such rich indulgence as this blessed, to be alive in this year of God's choice. The blessing is spread throughout the whole world and all the world is called to receive the badge of immortality."[59] But if this is the case, then the Crusade is a Jubilee open to everyone—not only to an elite but to all sinners. It is not merely a question of a challenge to noble knights: there is a terrible moral risk for anyone who refuses to take this unique opportunity.[60]

St. Bernard even more than Urban II believed that the Crusade was a providential opportunity for the total renewal of feudal society.

With exaltation and immense relief, the

first great army of repentant sinners started for the East, assured by Pope Urban himself that if they died on the expedition they would possess eternal life without further delay. "The robbers and pirates," said Oderic Vital, "criminals of every sort, moved by grace, came forth from the abyss of their wretchedness, disavowed their crimes and forsook them, and departed for the far-off country."[61]

Thus we see that in the course of time the peaceful and defenseless pilgrimage, the humble and meek "return to the source" of all life and grace, became the organized martial expedition to liberate the land promised to Abraham and his sons. It is surely significant that in the Middle Ages this conception of the Christian life became deeply embedded in European man: the "center," the "source," the "holy place," the "promised land," the "place of resurrection" becomes something to be attained, conquered, and preserved by politics and by force of arms. The whole Christian life and all Christian virtue then takes on a certain martial and embattled character. The true life of Christian virtue now becomes a struggle to death with pagan adversaries who are wickedly standing in the way of one's divinely appointed goal and perversely preventing fulfillment of a "manifest destiny."

Meanwhile, of course, certain ambiguities appeared in this conception of the Christian life as a mystique of martial and political organization. In the Second Crusade these ambiguities made themselves decisively felt: if the Crusade is a war to annihilate the enemy, then strategy comes first and the army should besiege Aleppo. If it is primarily a pilgrimage, then the crusading pilgrims should go up to Jerusalem. Yet the king had not made a vow to conquer Aleppo, only to go to Jerusalem.[62]

Thus, the concept of an essentially embattled Christian society tended to become inseparable from the Christian outlook, one might almost say the Christian faith. Christian eschatology in the West took on a very precise historical and social coloring in centuries of combat against the Turk. It was defense of Western Christendom against Eastern and pagan autocracy and power.

It would be naïve to underestimate the sincerity and the deep spiritual motivation of the Crusades, just as it would be naïve to ignore the fact that the violence, the greed, the lust, and the continued depravity of the worst elements continued unchanged. In point of fact, the Crusades had an immense effect on European and Christian society in the West. They certainly opened the way to renaissance and modern Christendom. But the paradise of spiritual benefits that had been hoped for was never attained. On the contrary, from the point of view of East-West relations in Christendom, the Crusades were a disaster. They certainly made all reunion between Rome and Constantinople unthinkable.

Above all, the Crusades introduced a note of fatal ambiguity into the concept of pilgrimage and penance. What was intended as a remedy for sins of violence, particularly murder, now became a consecration of violence. There is, of course, a distinction between war and murder, and the sacrifice entailed by warfare can certainly be regarded as "penitential." But a man prone to violence and passion, a potential or actual murderer and sadist, is not likely to make too many fine distinctions when he discovers that he can now not only kill people legitimately, but even offer his acts to God as "good works" and as "penance," provided he concentrates on infidels, regarded as the embodiment of all evil.

We know that the Crusaders did not confine their warlike activities to what was juridically "holy." The sack of Christian Constantinople and the internecine battles among the Crusaders themselves are there to prove it.

Finally, a very interesting development took place in the Crusades. The mystique of sacred love was, in the twelfth century, very close to the courtly love of the troubadours. But we find, curiously enough, that a typical troubadour, Jaufré Rudel, who took part in the Second Crusade, could sing in the same breath of the love for little Jesus in Bethlehem and of a more secular love for the "distant lady" in whose "service" the loyal knight will risk death and imprisonment. The Crusade becomes merged with the romance of courtly love. At the same time the sacred element tends to be neglected by those who, like Bertrand de Born, are engrossed in the martial glory and exploits of the knights.[63]

V

So much for the East. There remained the fabulous paradise of the West. It is curious that in the folklore tradition of Spain, the "Lost Island" of the West, identified with the Brendan legend to the point that it was given Brendan's own name, remained the paradisiacal refuge to which the kings of Spain and Portugal might flee from Moorish invasions,[64] just as in the Celtic legend the "land of promise" in the western ocean was evidently regarded as a place of refuge from the Norsemen.

Christopher Columbus was most probably aware of the Brendan legend[65] as well as of such classic medieval descriptions of the "Lost Island," or Perdita, as that of Honorius of Autun (or more exactly, William of Conches):

> There is a certain island of the Ocean called Perdita, and it excels all the lands of the earth in the beauty and fertility of all things. Found once by chance, it was later sought again and not found, whence it is called Perdita. To this isle, Brendan is said to have come.[66]

The description has all the mythical qualities of the lost paradise, and Columbus's idyllic description of his landfall on Hispaniola showed that the new land appeared to him to be in every way an earthly paradise. He did not believe he had discovered Perdita, however, and Spanish expeditions in search of the "Lost Island" continued even after the discovery of the American mainland.

Brendan's Island was marked ("tentatively") on maps as late as the eighteenth century.[67] It was even formally renounced by Portugal in the Treaty of Evora (1519), so that if it ever were found it was already assigned in advance (by the Apostolic See) to his Catholic majesty of Spain.

In one word, the Renaissance explorers, the conquistadores, the Puritans, the missionaries, the colonizers, and doubtless also the slave traders and pirates, were in their own way deeply influenced by the mythical paradisiacal aspect of the Americas. But it was a paradise into which they could not penetrate without the most profound ambiguities.

They came, in a way, as "penitents" or as men seeking renewal, deliverance from the past, the gift to begin again. But at the same time the pattern of this renewal forbade neither self-enrichment nor the free enjoyment of the opportunities which the "paradise" so generously offered (native women). And it prescribed, above all, as a sort of vestige of crusading ardor and as an earnest of absolution, an uncompromising zeal in the subjection of the infidel—and, of course, in his conversion. It was also a good thing to build churches at home with Inca gold. While St. Theresa of Avila was following her interior and mystic itinerary (not without some very energetic peregrination about Spain, founding Carmels[68]), her brother was in the Kingdom of Quito getting rich. When he returned to Spain, he financed the Carmel of Seville (where St. Theresa enjoyed the view of the river with the gallant ships of the Armada back from the Indies). And there is no reason to doubt the depth and sincerity of his inner life, troubled only by certain violent reactions, which his sister, though she had never experienced such things, did not find surprising.

There was in the Indies the lush and tempting beauty and fantastic opulence of nature. There were the true and legendary riches, from the mines of San Luis Potosí to the lake of Eldorado and the fountain of eternal youth. There were the Indians and their cities, appearing now as idyllic "noble savages" in utopian communities, now as treacherous devils indulging in infernal tricks and sunk in the worst forms of heathenism.

Thus, the European white man set foot on the shores of America with the conflicting feelings of an Adam newly restored to paradise and of a Crusader about to scale the walls of Acre.

The mentality of the pilgrim and that of the Crusader had fused together to create a singular form of alienation: that of the Puritan "pilgrim father" and that of the conquistador. Centuries of ardent, unconscious desire for the Lost Island had established a kind of right to paradise once it was found. It never occurred to the sixteenth-century Spaniard or Englishman to doubt for a moment that the new world was entirely and rightly his. It had been promised and given to him by God. It was the end of centuries of pilgrimage. It was the long-sought land of promise and renewal, where the old deficiencies and limitations no longer existed: the land of the new beginning not only for the individual but for society itself. The land of refuge from persecution. The land of peace and plenty, where all the iniquities and oppressions of the old world were forgotten. Here peace and unity were bought at the price of Christian courage in battling with the wilderness and with the infidel. To conquer and subjugate the native population was not regarded as an unjust aggression, as usurpation or as robbery and tyranny but on the contrary as proof of one's loyalty to all the values dear to the European and Christian heart since Charlemagne.

It is true, however, that some of the missioners had a different and more mystical view of paradise. But their solution was only more logically and consistently paradisiacal; as in the primitive and religious Jesuit utopias in Paraguay, or the communities of Vasco de Quiroga in Mexico.

These were, indeed, admirable and virtuous efforts. But for the greater part, the pilgrims were rushing upon the Lost Island with a combative ferocity and a wasteful irresponsibility that have tainted the fruits of the paradise tree with bitterness ever since.

Somehow it has been forgotten that a paradise that can be conquered and acquired by force is not paradise at all.

So the story of man's pilgrimage and search has reached the end of a cycle and is starting on another: now that it is clear that there is no paradise on earth that is not defiled as well as limited, now that there are no lost islands, there is perhaps some dry existentialist paradise of clean ashes to be discovered and colonized in outer space: a "new beginning" that initiates nothing and is little more than a sign of our irreversible decision to be disgusted with the paradises and pilgrimages of earth. Disgust with paradise, but not with crusades! The new planet is apparently to be the base for a more definitive extermination of infidels, together with the mass of less agile pilgrims so occupied in keeping body and soul together that they cannot be singled out as pilgrims to a promised land.

And yet the pilgrimage must continue, because it is an inescapable part of man's structure and program. The problem is for his pilgrimage to make sense—it must represent a complete integration of his inner and outer life, of his relation to himself and to other men.

The Bible has always taken man in the concrete, never in the abstract. The world has been given by God not to a theoretical man but to the actual beings that we are. If we instinctively seek a paradisiacal and special place on earth, it is because we know in our inmost hearts that the earth was given us in order that we might find meaning, order, truth, and salvation in it. The world is not only a vale of tears. There is joy in it somewhere. Joy is to be sought, for the glory of God.

But the joy is not for mere tourists. Our pilgrimage is more than the synthetic happy-making of a vacation cruise. Our journey is from the limitations and routines of "the given"—the *Dasein* which confronts us as we are born into it without choice— to the creative freedom of that love which is personal choice and commitment. Paradise symbolizes this freedom and creativity, but in reality this must be worked out in the human and personal encounter with the stranger seen as our other self.

As long as the Inca, the Maya, the Mestizo, the Negro, the Jew, or what have you, confronts us as *Dasein,* as a lump of limited and nonnegotiable *en-soi,* he will seem to stand in the way of our fulfillment. *"L'enfer, c'est les autres,"*[69] and we will seek paradise by combating his presence, subduing him, enslaving him, eliminating him.

Our task now is to learn that if we can voyage to the ends of the earth and there find *ourselves* in the aborigine who most differs from ourselves, we will have made a fruitful pilgrimage. That is why pilgrimage is necessary, in some shape or other. Mere sitting at home and meditating on the divine presence is not enough for our time. We have to come to the end of a long journey and see that the stranger we meet there is no other than ourselves—which is the same as saying that we find Christ in him.

For if the Lord is risen, as He said, He is actually or potentially alive in every man. Our pilgrimage to the Holy Sepulchre is our pilgrimage to the stranger who is Christ our fellow-pilgrim and our brother. There is no lost island merely for the individual. We are all pieces of the paradise isle, and we can find our Brendan's island only when we all realize ourselves together as the paradise which is Christ and His Bride, God, man, and Church.

It was in this spirit that St. Francis went on pilgrimage—on his own original kind of "crusade"—to meet the Soldan: as a messenger not of violence, not of arrogant power, but of humility, simplicity, and love.[70]

And it was in this spirit that Pope John XXIII wrote *Pacem in Terris*.

VIRGINITY AND HUMANISM IN THE WESTERN FATHERS

A SCHOLAR WITH a profound understanding of both antiquity and the Middle Ages has said that "every true humanism delights spontaneously in the world and in the book."[1] But if this statement is true, how can we seriously assert that there was ever any such thing as a "patristic humanism," or worse still, a "monastic humanism"?

The age of the Fathers, the age of the first monks, was, of course, an age in which "the world" was rejected with uncompromising and single-minded intensity of purpose. Also the monks were, it is often thought, hostile to study: if not to the study of Scripture, then at least to the study of the classics and the grammarians. Besides this, the term "humanism" is often associated in the popular mind with an anti-Christian humanism which summarily rejects the Church or even God, on the grounds that religious faith keeps man alienated, suppressing his deepest and most vital energies, and preventing his full human development as an individual and as a member of society. The very idea of humanism tends to acquire a flavor of impiety and irreligion.

But when we know the Fathers better, we see that a great deal depends on what one means by "the world." Certainly it has never been Christian to reject the "world" in the sense of the cosmos created by God, dwelt in by the Incarnate Word, sanctified by the presence and action of the Mystical Christ, and destined to be transformed with man in a new eschatological creation. In this sense, the Fathers took the deepest and most spontaneous delight in the world, and the early monks believed they could already see paradise again in the landscape around them, even though it might be the arid desert of Egypt. As for the "book," we know how the Fathers loved the Bible. We know too that they could not refrain from quoting the classics, even while commenting on the Bible.

The purpose of the present essay is to point out how the Latin Fathers, even though they may at times have felt a certain amount of personal conflict in their struggle to reconcile the reading of the classics with the meditation on the Word of God (and the case of Jerome's famous dream[2] is typical), were most uncompromising in their defense of basic human values. This defense is very clear and forthright in their writings to or about virgins.

Not that they always urged the "more illustrious portion of the flock of Christ"[3] to read Ovid. Far from it. Yet their concern for the education of Christian virgins, and for their full, integral formation in every aspect of a joyous and positive Christian life, reflects all that is deepest and best in the humanism of Christian antiquity. To this humanism of the Fathers we can always profitably return as to a pure source of the Christian spirit.

We must not narrow the idea of humanism to the mere study of the classics or of the liberal arts, though this study and the disciplines connected with it are certainly essential. True Christian humanism is the full flowering of the theology of the Incarnation. It is rooted in a totally new concept of man which grew out of the mystery of the union of God and man in Christ. Christian humanism is therefore much more than the humanism of the Stoa or of the Academy sprinkled with a few drops of holy water and made official by a Papal brief. It is the full realization of man's dignity and obligations as son of God, as image of God, created, regenerated, and transformed in the Word made Flesh.

In writing about the way Christian virgins should dress, St. Cyprian is not content to praise that *disciplina custos spei,* the external discipline which preserves the purity of the theological virtues within the soul.[4] Virginal purity, itself manifested by external modesty, is a spiritual light which proclaims the glory of the presence of Christ in a human temple. "Let us radiate the light of God and bear it everywhere in a pure and stainless body."[5] Therefore the question of modest dress, the use of makeup, or attendance at the public baths is more than a matter of personal decency and self-protective caution. The glory of

God and of Christ is involved. The virgin is the *illustrior portio gregis,* and we must note the implications of the "light-bearing" in the adjective *illustrior.* She not only bears the lamp of virtue and almsgiving (the light of the virgin's lamp is active charity), but she is herself a lamp kindled with the light of Christ. She is a more perfect replica of that image of God which is in all the "illuminated"—the baptized. The Church, the stainless Bride of Christ, cannot but concern herself more particularly with the purity of virgins since that purity is her own glory. The purity of the virgin is closely connected with the purity of the faith itself.[6] It is the purity of truth. The virgin is what a redeemed human person really ought to be. Hence, a twofold reason why she should not use cosmetics: on the one hand, if she paints her face she transforms it into a lie, making it other than God wanted it to be. This of course is a trope even in secular satire. But the meaning here is deeper. She in a certain sense yields up the freedom of the children of God and returns to what St. Paul would call captivity under the "elements of this world" (Gal. 4:3) since she implicitly wants to be desired with an erotic love. But the realm of *eros* is also the realm of death.

The house of Hymen and of pleasure is also, unfortunately, the house of cruel pain. The wife in the ancient world was more or less the husband's property, a thing rather than a person, and she was not always treated with gentleness or consideration.[7] The virgin was by her consecration liberated by Christ from the tyranny of a pagan or half-converted husband.

Hence, the virgin had an obligation to preserve the eschatological freedom, which enabled her to manifest in the world, in a really prophetic witness, the future state of glory promised to all the baptized. "Be precisely what God your maker made you; be such as the Father's hand created you. Keep an uncorrupted face, a pure neck, a form without adulteration," says St. Cyprian,[8] and adds, above all: "Keep, O virgins, keep what you have begun to be, keep that which you will one day be. That which we will all be you have begun to be. You have already laid hold on the glory of the resurrection even in this present life."[9]

The eschatological humanism of Christian virginity as understood by St. Cyprian is therefore not the mere denial of the world, of love, and of man. It is the conquest and transformation of man and the world in the divinizing power of the resurrection. It is the victory of Christ over suffering, anguish, misery, and the whole realm of death of which sexual love is but a part.

It must not be forgotten that the Fathers also saw in virginity the return to the paradisiacal perfection of man's beginning, the recovery of the innocence, the purity, and the familiarity with God for which man was originally created. St. Ambrose says that "in the sacred virgins we see on earth that angelic life which we once lost in Paradise."[10] St. Jerome[11] adds that if married life is appropriate to man after the fall, the virginal life is characteristic of Paradise. In a word, virginity is man's "normal" state, a state of personal and spiritual freedom above the vicissitudes of terrestrial existence, which is always lived in the shadow of death and in which sex provides a means of survival, not for the person, but only for human nature. Christian virginity is therefore the highest affirmation of human values and aspirations, for it is the liberation and fulfillment of the human person in union with God in Christ.

II

Demetrias, a daughter of Roman aristo-
crats who had fled from the sack of Rome
into North Africa and had there, to the
consternation of the whole Roman world,
suddenly renounced a brilliant marriage in
order to consecrate her life to Christ, was
praised by Jerome for her courageous as-
sertion of *Christian liberty*.[12] In defying the
possible censure of her parents (who, as a
matter of fact, fully approved her resolu-
tion) and of society (which, at any rate,
wondered at it), Demetrias had followed
the footsteps of the virgin martyr Agnes.
Jerome evokes the savage turmoil of Rome
in flames, echoing with the cries of women
violated by Barbarians. He recalls the ob-
scene nuptial lampoons sung at wed-
dings.[13] The "Fescenninan Songs" represent the victory of lust, the triumph of
unregenerate nature and indeed of the

Prince of this world asserting his power over all flesh. But the Christian virgin conquers the flesh and her victory is the victory of Christ. Jerome exults over the triumph of Christ in the purity of Demetrias. Again, here is the theme of divine truth shining gloriously in the liberty of the virgin who asserts her freedom against the insistence of the flesh and the tyrannical demands of social convention.

If we look closely, then, at the idea of "the world" in these patristic writings on virginity, we see that it is always the corrupt pagan society in which human love and honor tend to be debased. The virgin is one who conquers this debased and confused society precisely because she not only has the grace of Christ but unites with it supreme human qualities of soul and body. By no means will Jerome consent to the practice of certain unfortunate parents (*miseri parentes*) who, weak in

Christian faith, consecrate to God only the daughters who will never be able to attract a husband.[14]

St. Ambrose, in his succinct little tract *De Institutione Virginis*[15] (On the Education of a Virgin), blends mysticism and humanism together in a manner that merits a much more detailed study than we can attempt here. The full maturity of the Christian life is attained in a virginal union with Christ which itself implies *the perfect integration of the whole human person.* Union with Christ implies His entrance into a personality which is perfectly united in all its three traditional elements of body, soul, and spirit—*corpus, anima, spiritus.*[16]

This treatise of St. Ambrose's is particularly interesting for its outspoken defense of women in general. Basing himself on the creation narrative of Genesis, and on St. Paul's doctrine of the mystery of Christ typified in the union of Adam and Eve, the mystical humanism of Ambrose declares that man without woman is physically and spiritually incomplete, and that woman is in a very deep sense the "glory" of man, his spiritual completion, his "grace," without whom he cannot fully possess or recover his true being in Christ.

Indeed, man was made of the earth, but woman was made of man as a kind of figure of that grace which Christ came to bring,[17] a figure of spiritual life and of the Church.

We are therefore far from the pessimism of Augustine. On the contrary, St. Ambrose vehemently exonerates Eve of full responsibility in the fall of man: she was deceived by a superior being, and man, deceived by her, his inferior, is therefore without excuse![18] With Eve, original sin was error: with Adam, it was sin, and Adam's fault exculpates Eve from all guilt, since he is the more responsible. Not only that, but the penalty of childbearing in suffering is for the good of Eve and it washes away, in salutary penance, the sin of Adam.[19]

We seem to be contradicting what was just said by Jerome: that childbearing is something to be dreaded and avoided. Ambrose goes deeper: but in doing so he takes a deeply compassionate and optimistic view of woman. He defends woman against the brutal self-complacency of man, who blames her for everything and curses her as a stumbling block and temptation to him, whereas all the while it is man himself who seeks in woman that which tempts him.[20] The beauty of woman's body is a great work of God, meant to be a sign of that far greater interior beauty, the special clarity and loveliness of her spirit.[21] Indeed, St. Ambrose declares, it is quite evident that women are more generous, more virtuous, more self-sacri-ficing than men.[22]

Finally, in an astute observation upon Abraham's rather cowardly lie that Sarah was his sister (Genesis 20:2), Ambrose remarks that in fact Sarah was the glory of Abraham, and implies that she was far better than Abraham deserved.

This totally refreshing defense of woman gives us some indication of the depth and reality of patristic humanism. Indeed, how can there be a true "humanism" when half of the human race is ignored or excluded? Pagan humanism, the exclusive preserve of man, only exalts his complacency and justifies his selfishness with a veneer of philosophy. A humanism for men only is, as we have seen, nothing but a barbarous falsehood. The light of true humanism is kindled by the Incarnate Word.

It may be mentioned here in passing

that St. Ambrose's *De Institutione Virginis* devotes many columns to the praise of Mary's virginity and to the defense of her virginal motherhood. Mary is indeed the model of all Christian virgins, as well as the crown and glory of all women. Indeed, Ambrose's glorification of women is to be understood in the light of the mystery of the virginal Mother of God.

In the life of the Christian virgin, the mystery of Mary's motherhood is reproduced spiritually and in a hidden manner. Just as Mary was the "door" by which Christ entered the world even though the door was not "opened," so too the virgin is filled with a love which is rich in material gifts, which generously gives itself everywhere in outward works of mercy, yet at the same time never yields its interior secret, which remains totally consecrated to God. The Christian virgin is, like Mary, a *porta clausa,* a "closed door" (cf. Ezechiel

46:1–2). In bodily things, she gives but does not receive human love and consolation. In spiritual things, she receives from God but does not reveal the secret communicated to her by the King. Thus, her life is integrated in a perfectly ordered love. God is loved for His own sake, and the neighbor purely and disinterestedly for the love of God.[23]

Here precisely we come to the question of the study of the word of God in the contemplative life of the Christian virgin.

There can be no question that this contemplative life has both an intellectual and a mystical aspect. The two necessarily go together. The contemplative life of the Christian virgin is centered on a deep interior meditation of the word of God, which itself leads to union with the Person of the Word. This meditation begins of course with a reading of the sacred text, which must be fully understood both in its literal and in its spiritual senses.[24] In actual fact, it is Christ Himself who opens to his virginal spouse the sense of the Scriptures in secret. It is in the word of the Scriptures that He comes secretly to her, and enters into her heart as He once entered secretly through the "closed door" of the Blessed Virgin's womb.

St. Ambrose says: "Thou are a closed door, O Virgin. Let no one open thy door once locked by the Holy One and True Who has the key of David, who opens and no one closes, who closes and no one opens: HE HAS OPENED TO THEE THE SCRIPTURES, LET NO ONE CLOSE THEM. HE HAS CLOSED THY PURITY, LET NO ONE OPEN IT."[25] A beautiful text, which shows clearly the intimate connection between virginity of body and purity of heart,[26] integrity of body and unadulterated faith, chastity in the flesh and mystical love in the spirit.

Needless to say, the spiritual understanding of the sacred text implies a certain intellectual preparation. Therefore, the virginal life certainly requires study and education, of the kind which we generally term "humanistic." However, the virginal life is not merely a life of pious study. The purpose of intellectual preparation is to open the way to receive the mystical fire like that which Elias breathed into the dead child. The fire of mystical understanding is the guarantee of virginal purity being preserved. "Keep this fire with thee in thy heart, it will revive thee, lest the coldness of perpetual death steal in and take possession of thee."[27] But between the study of the text and its mystical understanding comes a very important intermediary stage which is the chief activity of the virgin: the rumination of the sacred text in meditation. This is her "world," in which she lives and moves and has her being. The Scriptures are the Paradise she has received in exchange for the society of men. "Once dead to the world I beg thee not to touch the things of time lest thou be contaminated by them: but at all times in psalms and hymns and spiritual canticles withdraw thyself from the society of this world, singing to God and not to man. Do as holy Mary did, and meditate on these words in thy heart. And like a good little lamb, ruminate in thy mouth the divine precepts."[28]

III

St. Jerome insists that his virgins and widows keep assiduously to their reading. If they have embraced the life of Mary instead of that of Martha, this means precisely that they are intent on *doctrina* (learning)[29] rather than on labor, though of course manual work too will always have its essential part to play in their lives.[30] Eustochium must keep at her reading and learn all she can: *crebrius lege, disce quamplurima.*[31] However, the pious trope of Jerome and so many other patristic authors, including Ailred of Rievaulx,[32] about "falling asleep on the sacred page"[33] is not exactly the most convincing witness to patristic humanism. It has a certain element of ambiguity about it!

One might ask if the Christian virgin ought to read the Latin classics. St. Jerome anticipates this question from Eustochium and answers with an emphatic "no." She should not want to appear learned in the pagan classics, nor should she waste her time trying to write lyric poems in the ancient meters, reciting them among other learned matrons in affected tones; for "What consent can there be between Christ and Belial? What has Horace to do with the Psalter? Virgil with the Gospels?

Cicero with the Apostle?"[34] And here Jerome reveals the horrible example of his own temptation and fall, the famous Ciceronian vision, in which he appears before the judgment seat of Christ, is asked what kind of a thing he claims to be, and when he replies "a Christian" he is rebuked: "Thou liest, thou art not a Christian but a Ciceronian, for where thy treasure is there thy heart is also."[35]

This, as we know, was no small crisis in Jerome's life. He had collapsed in Syria, and the monastic brethren, taking him for dead, were preparing his obsequies. The immediate cause of the collapse seems to have been the intense struggle over the classics, for he was completely unable to relinquish Cicero and Plautus even in the desert.

In his vision, having received some kind of mystical flagellation, he vowed never again to touch a pagan book.

Unfortunately, or rather perhaps fortunately, we find him a few columns later in Migne writing to Marcella on textual problems of Scripture and quoting Horace in mockery of those "two-legged asses" who, instead of agreeing with Jerome's improved translation, persist in clinging to the old familiar versions.[36]

It is well known that Jerome did not keep this "vow" never to read Cicero. But quite apart from the classics, we can see from the letters he wrote on technical Scriptural questions to his virginal correspondents that he expected them to have rather sharp intellects well prepared by thorough study to appreciate the meaning of what he was telling them.

Without going into all of Jerome's ideas about the education of virgins, let us simply examine the charming letter to Laeta in which the old scholar of Bethlehem sketches out a program for the training of a small child, little Paula, the niece of Eustochium and the granddaughter of St. Paula, so that she might grow up to be a truly "wise virgin." Here it is a question of a very special training because the child had been consecrated to God even before her birth. This suggests that her parents should keep in mind the model of St. John the Baptist. In any case, little Paula must never hear anything, never say anything, except what pertains to the fear of God. But let us be quite clear what this means. Not only is Paula to be protected from vicious influences, but she is also to be guarded against bad Latin. She must learn to speak correctly from the very first, "lest she should learn in tender years what must be unlearned later."[37] She must not acquire the vice of careless diction, which might be contracted by babytalk in the nursery. No, even in early childhood she must learn to speak clearly and correctly. No fault of speech is to be regarded as slight.

Furthermore, she might as well begin her Greek while she is still in early childhood.

The passage where Jerome speaks of Paula learning her letters by playing with ivory blocks with the letters carved on them[38] needs no comment here. It is doubtless inspired by Quintilian. Paula of course learns to speak by lisping the "sweet psalms": *adhuc tenera lingua psalmis dulcibus imbuatur.*[39] It is interesting to notice that Jerome anticipates modern educational psychology when he declares that Paula must first learn by playing and that learning must always be pleasurable to her. It is of the greatest importance, says Jerome, to *see that she never comes to hate study.* A consecrated virgin would, according to his way of thinking, be terribly handicapped if in early childhood she acquired a bitter dislike of learning which she could never shake off in riper years. *Cavendum est in primis ne oderit studia, ne amaritudo eorum praecepta in infanita ultra*

75

rudes annos transeat.[40] For this reason she should not come to associate study with punishment. She should be encouraged with rewards.

Passing over the details of Paula's spiritual formation, which is described in all the familiar and traditional language of asceticism, and recalls St. Cyprian, we come to Jerome's plan for her Scripture studies.

First of all, the child must learn not only to read Scripture daily but to give a daily account of her *lectio.*[41] Memory of course plays a very important part. She will learn parts of the Scripture by heart, not only in Latin but also in Greek.[42] At the same time she will go to church, to the "Temple of her true Father," along with her parents (never with a boy friend),[43] and there she will listen intently to the reading of the Sacred Books, realizing that it is the voice of her Spouse calling her to marriage with Him. This will help her to be deaf to the attractions of worldly music and friendships.

Her reading of Scripture is closely integrated with prayer,[44] which is to be taught by a "veteran virgin," a *virgo veterana* (a term which must not suggest a military image to our minds).

Her prayers are those of the canonical hours. She will rise in the night for "orations and psalms." She will sing hymns at daybreak (lauds). At tierce, sext, and none, she will stand in the battle line like a warrior of Christ. When the lamp is lit, she will render the evening sacrifice.[45] Prayer and Scripture study are also integrated with her manual work. She will work with her hands, spinning wool and weaving. And she will not waste her time on silks or other fine materials, but the Scripture will take the place of silks and riches in her life.[46]

Her Scripture reading will of course follow a special plan. We have already seen that in earliest childhood she learns to speak with the very words of the Psalter. Jerome returns to this in his *ratio studiorum:* "Let her first learn the Psalter, and in the Proverbs of Solomon let her be taught to live." After that, in an order which suggests Origen but which eventually differ from him in important details, she will learn, in Ecclesiastes, "to trample down the things of this world." At the same time she will follow the examples of virtue and patience given in the Book of Job. Then she will pass on to the Gospels, "never to let them out of her hands," and she will with all the "will of her heart drink in the Acts of the Apostles and the Epistles." "When she shall have filled the storerooms of her heart with these riches, she will commit to memory the Prophets, the Heptateuch, the Book of

Kings and Chronicles as well as the volumes of Esdras and Esther."[47]

We note the language of this passage. *Mandet memoriae* tells us that the terms *discat* and *cordis sui cellarium his opibus locupletare* all mean the same thing. She is to make the Sacred Books part of her very being, to treasure them in her heart and in her memory so that they fill her thoughts at all times. This was a most important aspect of the education of virgins and of monks in the early days of the Church, and remained so down until the invention of printing.

When she has learned all the rest of the Scriptures, then it will be time for her to come without danger to the Canticle of Canticles.[48]

Thus, we see that for St. Jerome the virginal life, centered on the word of God, is a harmonious and well integrated whole which culminates in the highest spiritual union, but which begins nevertheless with simple respect for spoken Latin. It is instructive to see how, for St. Jerome, there is no division, no discontinuity in this conception of the spiritual life. It begins with the fullest respect for the ordinary spoken word. It continues with the study of language, with the memorization of the inspired word of God, the constant meditation of that word, in an attitude of greater and greater interior attentiveness to the Word Himself Who speaks in the Scriptures, until at last He reveals Himself in a spiritual and personal way to His chosen one, and unites her to Himself.

IV

In résumé, we have here a perfect and integral Christian humanism. It guards against an inordinate taste for pagan poetry and myth, but it nevertheless does not really exclude anything essential to the purest tradition of Christian humanism. On the contrary, Jerome's plan of education for little Paula is simply a Christian adaptation and development of classical educational ideas as they were inherited from Cicero and Quintilian. Cassiodorus reminds us that Quintilian's idea of rhetoric could be summed up as a training "which takes a good man, expert in speech, from his earliest childhood, through a course of training in all the arts and disciplines of noble letters, as the need of the whole commonwealth calls for such a man to defend it."[49]

The Christian virgin is by no means an orator, but she is dedicated to a life of praise, in divinely inspired words which transcend human eloquence. Her praise is not the defense of civil right, but the proclamation of the freedom of the Sons of God in the Risen Christ. She nevertheless needs training in the essentials of those same "arts and disciplines of noble letters" which help her to understand and use human speech as a divinely given instrument. She will rise above the merely human use of this instrument, and carry it to a spiritual and angelic level, for her life of praise is one with the life of the angels in heaven, and is therefore a higher kind of communication.

On this highest level, it is no longer the consecrated virgin alone who speaks, praises, and sings: it is Christ Himself, her Spouse, who acts, thinks, speaks, and utters praise in her. As St. Ambrose puts it: "In all her senses and actions, Christ shines forth, Christ is her aim, Christ Himself speaks."[50]

In Laeta's family there was an old pagan grandfather, still clinging to the past, sour and bitter over the decline of the great culture of Greece and Rome, and still disdaining to submit to the new faith which all his family had now embraced. Yet he loved little Paula, and Jerome (who may perhaps have somehow identified his own rude Ciceronian self with the surly grandfather) advises in a flash of wise spontaneity: "When [Paula] sees her grandfather, let her leap into his arms, let her cling to his neck, and whether he likes it or not, let her sing Alleluia into his ears."[51]

Surely, this is one of the most apt and perfect expressions of the true relation between the humanism of Christianity and that of the ancient classical world! In any case, it represents the final solution of Jerome's own conflict.

THE ENGLISH MYSTICS

THE LAST FEW YEARS have seen the publication of important studies on the English mystics, together with new modern versions of their writings. The present essay grew out of a review article on the more important studies printed in 1961. When the essay was submitted to *Jubilee,* where it first appeared, someone who read the manuscript remarked that he had never even known there were English mystics. It is therefore high time for all these studies and new versions to appear, and a brief introduction to the subject of English mysticism will obviously not be superfluous.

There is every reason for interest in the English mystics. They have a charm and simplicity that are unequaled by any other school. And they are also, it may be said, generally quite clear, down-to-earth, and practical, even when they are concerned with the loftiest of matters. They never seem to have thought of their life with God as something recondite or even unusual. They were simply Christians. They rejoiced to know in Christ their Creator and Redeemer. They rejoiced that in Him they had direct access to the Father of Lights.

This study, while mentioning Thomas Traherne, whose *Centuries of Meditations* also appeared in 1961, concentrates on the Roman Catholic mystics, especially those of the fourteenth century. There is no doubt that it would be important to discuss the spirituality of the seventeenth-century Anglican school, the Cambridge

Platonists, the Friends, the Methodists. But the difficulties and complications of such a study make it impossible in a short essay. Suffice it to say that in William Law or Isaac Pennington one can certainly find echoes of the great fourteenth-century tradition, which was itself, as we state in the conclusion to this essay, the fruit of the English medieval monastic spirituality.

ENGLISH SPIRITUALITY

Cardinal Newman was too Catholic to be anything but an English Catholic. His Catholic instinct told him that universality did not demand renunciation of his English outlook and spiritual heritage. Hence, he did not follow the more romantic converts of his time. Or rather, though he was momentarily influenced by them, it was just long enough to discover with alarm that he could be untrue to himself and to his authentic sense of the English tradition. Having once wavered in the presence of the overcompensation practiced by some of his colleagues, for whom nothing was sufficiently un-English, or too aggressively Roman, he drew back in salutary fear from the abyss of exotic and baroque clichés into which he saw himself about to fall headlong. He preserved the simplicity of his English devotion, and the clarity of the English spiritual idiom.

The English mystics belong to the ancient, patristic tradition, which Newman loved and which was so thoroughly transplanted into Britain by the early monks as to become authentically part of the very essence of the English spirit. Unfortunately, at the Reformation, the mystics were forgotten by all but a few of the old English Catholics, mostly in exile. When Catholic and mystical piety returned once again to England, it was in an alien and baroque costume, so that it appeared suspicious, theatrical, and false in the English setting. Post-Reformation continental terminology, transliterated into cumbersome jargon, did not slip easily and naturally off the English tongue. Its attitudes seemed forced and artificial. But the more uncomfortable the piety of the continental Counter Reformation appeared to the new English convert, the more he thought it his duty to sacrifice his native realism and soundness of taste, submitting to what secretly appalled him: thus, "nature" bowed to the "supernatural," *ad majorem Dei gloriam.* It was the Protestants and Anglicans of the nineteenth century who rediscovered the English mystics.

But that which most genuinely glorifies God is a catholicity true enough to respect the manifold variety of races, nations, and traditions which seek their fulfillment and their *raison d'être* in Christ. Our natures do not manifest Him by being suppressed but by being transfigured by obedience to the Gospel. Just as Christ came to fulfill the Law, not to destroy it, so too He came to fulfill the authentic aspirations of the customs, traditions, and philosophies of the Greeks and "Gentiles" in general. Catholicism should then be English in England, not Italian; Chinese in China and not French; African in Africa, not Belgian. The loss of the English mystical tradition would be, in fact, irreparable. The strength, sincerity, simplicity, and naturalness of an authentic English sense would be stifled. What has perhaps happened, with the loss of the earthy and humorous naturalness of medieval English piety, has been a slow smothering of the English religious instinct, and its final reduction to a lay and despairing state of tongue-tied agnosticism.

Who were the English mystics? The

custom has been to designate, by this name, the greatest and most characteristic of them, the fourteenth-century contemplatives, who first developed a mysticism that was purely in the English idiom, expressed in the rich original vernacular of their time. This pure "English school" includes four great figures above all: Richard Rolle, Walter Hilton, Julian (i.e., Juliana) of Norwich, and the author of the *Cloud of Unknowing,* whom no one has ever been able to identify. Sometimes, as in the study of the English mystics by Professor David Knowles,[1] the sixteenth-century Benedictine Dom Augustine Baker is added to this group, since he is more or less in the fourteenth-century tradition, being insular and original, a decidedly solitary and independent spirit. But one might also include some of the great medieval mystics, who, though they wrote in Latin, were distinctly English in their character: St. Ailred of Rievaulx, for instance, and Adam the Carthusian (of Witham), or the anonymous Monk Solitary of Farne.[2] A recent anthology[3] has decided to take this approach, and it contains selections from the medieval mystics only. The four great mystics of the fourteenth-century school are represented there, together with Margery Kempe, St. Ailred of Rievaulx, and St. Edmund Rich, Archbishop of Canterbury. The texts of Ailred and Edmund have never been available before in English, and are typical examples of the medieval Augustinian tradition.

Ailred of Rievaulx was a twelfth-century Cistercian abbot, friend and disciple of St. Bernard of Clairvaux, father of one of the great monastic families that peopled the valleys of Yorkshire and built the pure and severe churches whose ruins still amaze even the most hardened tourist. For Ailred, as for all his fellow Cistercians,

these monasteries were "schools of charity" (*scholae caritatis*). Following the Augustinian tradition, the Cistercians taught
that man was made in God's image in the
sense that he was created for pure love,
but he had fallen from the divine likeness
by centering all his love upon himself. The
monastery and monastic life were designed
to reeducate and reform man's capacity to
love, liberating him from fixation upon
himself, teaching him to love the divine
image in his fellow man, and finally leading
him to love perfectly, in spirit and in
truth, by returning to the source of love,
God Himself. Such is the theme of Ailred's
principal work, the "Mirror of Charity"
(*Speculum Caritatis*).

This ascent to purity begins with ascetic
labor but terminates in the repose of contemplation, the "Sabbath" of perfect love,
in which God is now not only believed and

known but also experienced in mystical wisdom.

But Ailred's doctrine of contemplation must be seen in the context of the cenobitic tradition. In the cloister, the monks share with one another the fruits of contemplation, not by preaching to one another, but by a spiritual friendship that bears witness to the presence of Christ in their midst. For Ailred, contemplation was shared in fraternal love, and his most original work is perhaps his dialogue *De Spirituali Amicitia* — in which the theme of Christian friendship is developed as a mystique of contemplative community life.

The best modern study of St. Ailred is unfortunately not yet available in English: it is a thesis by Father Amedée Hallier, O.C.S.O.,[4] which stresses the humanistic aspect of Ailred's thought, in its deep respect for the full integral reality of the human person, finally attained by a paradoxical stripping off of "self" and a fullness of pure love in Christ.

The mystics of the Middle Ages are not the only English contemplatives, however, and one could think of other writers that might fill out the picture. Some of them would perhaps not be as orthodox as Rolle, Hilton, and the Lady Julian: for instance, William Blake. Then there is the gentle and happy spirit of the Anglican Thomas Traherne, whose *Centuries*[5] has recently been published. He is certainly one of the most English and most paradisiacal of contemplative poets.

Hilda Vaughan, in her introduction to the *Centuries,* has rightly pointed out the close affinity of spirit between Traherne and Julian of Norwich. Both alike are enlightened by an innocence and joy that are not of this world. Both see the world with a simplicity and a wisdom given only by the Holy Spirit. This does not mean, how-

ever, that Traherne is altogether a child.
He is absorbed in ontological concerns, he
abounds in metaphysical conceits. He can
speak in theological symbols that echo the
intuitions of Julian of Norwich about the
Redemption:

> You never enjoy the world aright till the
> sea itself floweth in your veins, till you
> are clothed with the heavens and
> crowned with the stars; and perceive
> yourself to be the sole heir of the whole
> world, and more then so, because men
> are in it who are every one sole heirs as
> well as you.[6]

He can also be more difficult, more philosophical:

> By this you may know that you are infi-
> nitely beloved: God hath made your
> spirit a center in eternity comprehend-

ing all, and filled all about you in an endless manner with infinite riches: which
shine before you and surround you with
divine and heavenly enjoyments.[7]

In either case, what is important is not a
theory, not an abstract proposition, but a
concrete experience, expressed now in the
context of theological mystery, now in
philosophical language. Yet in every case
we must penetrate immediately to the
central intuition, a basic Eucharistic and
primitive Christian theology of praise:

By an act of the understanding therefore
be present now with all the creatures
among whom you live; and hear them in
their beings and operations praising God
in a heavenly manner. Some of them vo-
cally, others in their ministry, all of them
naturally and continually.

And he adds a sentence that manifests the real inner spirit of the English mystics in all their love of the positive and of the concrete:

> We infinitely wrong ourselves by laziness and confinement. All creatures in all nations and tongues and peoples praise God infinitely: and the more for being your sole and perfect treasures. You are never what you ought till you go out of yourself and walk among them.[8]

One of the later representatives of the tradition of the *Cloud of Unknowing* is the Capuchin Benet of Canfield, who, however, wrote mostly in Latin and French. Early translations of his *Rule of Perfection* exist, but they are not yet easily accessible. A critical edition is, we hope, soon to be published, and it will draw this little-known contemplative out of the obscurity in which he has lain hidden.

Born of Puritan gentry in Essex in 1562, William Flich went to London to read for the bar and was baptized a Catholic in 1585 by an imprisoned priest in one of the London jails. He then went to France and entered the Capuchin novitiate in 1587. There he took the name of Benet (or Benedict). Later, after a short period of imprisonment in England, he was guardian and novice master in the Capuchins, and died in 1610, regarded as a saint. Henri Brémond has a very high opinion of Benet, of whom he says: "Master of the masters themselves, of Berulle, Mme. Acarie, Marie de Beauvillier and many others, he in my opinion more than any other gave our French religious renaissance this clearly mystical character."

Benet's *Rule of Perfection* is a treatise on self-emptying by total abandonment to the will of God. Unfortunately, his treatment breaks the spiritual life up into divisions and subdivisions which bewilder more than they enlighten. He distinguishes between the *Active Life,* in which one obeys the "exterior will of God" and practices vocal prayer; the *Contemplative Life,* in which the "interior will of God" moves the contemplative from within, and prayer is totally simplified. Finally, and this is characteristic of Benet, there is the *Supereminent Life* transcending both action and contemplation in union with the "essential will of God." This is the life of the saint and the mystic, in "perfect unclothing of the Spirit." Benet's emphasis (and this is still a matter of questioning and controversy) is on the total cessation of all natural activity, and complete subjection to the divine movement "between two extremes of false rest and hurtful working," to "live constantly in the Infinite of the Divine Being and the nothingness of things."

This is of course not a pure negation. The "unclothing of the Spirit" is at the same time an illumination in "such an abundance of light that [the spirit] is clothed therewith as with a garment, transformed into it and made one with the light itself."[9]

Without further discussion of these later figures, let us concentrate our attention on the mystics of the fourteenth century and Dom Augustine Baker.

THE ENGLISH MYSTICS OF THE FOURTEENTH CENTURY

The fourteenth century was a period of disruption and new growth: the age of the Hundred Years' War, of the Black Death, of Joan of Arc, Langland, Dante, Occam. It was the age of Chaucer, when the spires of Norwich and Salisbury first soared into the hazy blue sky and when men first began to talk and write in the English tongue about God, love and prayer, work and war, rights and justice. In the fourteenth century, the Catholic spirit became fully, joyously, and outspokenly English. With the newfound vernacular piety, the solitary self-reliance of the hermits, the growth of independent spirit among the burghers and peasantry, there developed a kind of spontaneity and forthrightness, a courageous frankness mingled with humor which are characteristic of England. All these traits are found in the English mystics, whose humility is witty, whose ardor is simple and direct, and whose love for God is the whole offering of their complete self, not divided and destroyed but unified and transfigured in "self-naughting" and abandonment to His infinite mercy.

The mystics flourished above all in Yorkshire, the East Midlands, and East Anglia: lands of moors, of rolling wooded hills, or of vast fens laid out under a huge dome of blue sky. Rolle, the Oxford clerk who became a hermit in Yorkshire, is one of the first English vernacular poets. His is a genius of fire and light—and we shall see that for this very reason Knowles tends to question his mysticism. He is a lively and fervent poet for whom the experience of God is essentially "song and sweetness." Another hermit was the anonymous author of the *Cloud.* There is less fire in him that in Rolle, and less sweetness, but no less humor and a great deal more of the hard reality of dark contemplation. Hilton, too, had perhaps lived as a solitary before joining the Austin Canons at Thurgarton. His *Scale of Perfection,* of all the works of the English mystics, comes closest to being a treatise in the tradition of the Fathers, embracing the whole scope of the active and contemplative lives, the first being a "reformation of faith" and the second a "reformation of feeling," that is, of inner experience.

Hilton develops the traditional theology of the restoration, in Christ, of man's "lost likeness" to the divine image. Christ came to rescue man from a state of "forgetfulness and ignorance of God and monstrous love of himself." It is possible that Hilton was following Ailred of Rievaulx in his distinction between the image partially restored "in faith" and that more perfectly restored "in feeling," that is, in contemplative experience. But, in any event, the treatment is common to the medieval writers in the tradition of St. Augustine.

The *Scale of Perfection* is a "ladder" and hence it has steps or degrees, but Hilton, in this more characteristically English than Benet of Canfield, does not insist too much on analyzing and measuring out the precise stages through which the spiritual man is assumed to pass, on his way to mystical union. Hilton has too much respect for the existential realities of the spiritual life to violate their integrity by formal schematization.

He is at once more theological and less poetic than Rolle, and when he warns against attachment to "sounds or sweet savour or any other sensation" in mystical experience, he was quite probably reacting directly against the popularity of Rolle's poetic fervor, which may perhaps have appealed inordinately to the imagination and to the emotions of untrained beginners.

Detachment from a craving to "see" and "experience" divine things in a crude or human manner is then part of the "reformation of feeling," which is completed when one has attained to a purity of love that no longer reflects on itself or desires anything for itself. But this cannot be attained without a long, difficult struggle with that "obscure and heavy image of your own soul which has neither light to know God nor affection to love Him."[10]

THE CLOUD OF UNKNOWING

Although he is anonymous, the author of the *Cloud of Unknowing* is no less arresting a personality than any of the other English mystics. His voice has the same ring of sincerity and humor, of frankness, discretion, and sobriety. He is at once more learned, more sophisticated, and more shrewd than Rolle, who is not always moderate. The author of the *Cloud* is a professional in the tradition of "dark contemplation" that reached Europe from the Orient and flourished in the fourteenth century, especially in the Rhineland. The author of the *Cloud* invites comparison with Eckhart, whose influence he must have felt. The brilliant metaphysical improvisations of the Master of Rhenish mysticism and his bold figures of speech are not for the author of the *Cloud*. He speaks in quieter tones, for a strictly limited audience, in a doctrine too unassuming to make enemies. The *Cloud* of course quotes Pseudo-Dionysius—and this is practically the only one of the Fathers it quotes at all. The author even wrote a commentary on the *Mystical Theology* ("Hid Divinity") of the Areopagite. This book is, then, representative of the pure Dionysian tradition and has little in it of Augustinian speculation.

The thing that is most striking, perhaps, about the *Cloud of Unknowing* is the serene and practical assurance with which the author speaks of the "work" that he proposes to his hermit disciple. This is not merely a way of prayer, a manner of devotion: it is a *way of life*. It is a rare grace, a life to which one can only be called by God. It is not so much an exalted way as a rare one: rare by its very simplicity. It implies a peculiar sense of responsibility, a special gift of humility, an unusual common sense. It does not demand peculiar intellectual gifts, or unusual natural aptitudes. But it does require a special fidelity and, one might say, an extraordinary spiritual tact. It is a way of life (we call it, by way of cliché, the "contemplative life"), in which one must learn to act by not acting and to know by not knowing: to have one desire alone which is not really a desire but a kind of desirelessness, an openness, a habitual freedom in the sense of self-abandonment, a realization that all God asks is "that you turn your attention to Him, and then let Him alone. You must only guard the windows and doors for flies and enemies who may intrude. And if you willingly do this, then you will need only

to speak quietly and humbly in prayer and
soon He will help you."[11] Later, the author adds that this speaking in prayer says
little or nothing: and one of the chief preoccupations of the disciple led into the
"cloud" is to bear down upon understanding and put aside clear ideas and definite
wishes in order to attend, in perfect mindfulness, to the God who is not seen and
not known:

> Think of nothing but God Himself, so
> that nothing will work in your mind or
> in your will but only God Himself. You
> must then do whatever will help you to
> forget all the beings whom God has cre-
> ated, and all their works . . .[12]

This would seem to be the exact oppo-
site of the paragraph we quoted earlier
from Traherne. But are Traherne and the
Cloud really so far apart? In mysticism, op-

posites tend to meet and coincide, for the realm of spiritual experience is no longer the realm of strict logic in which A and not-A are irreconcilably set apart and opposed. In point of fact, it is by forgetting the immediate data of sense and letting go all preoccupation with material concerns that one enters into the kind of cosmic fellowship and unity with all beings that Traherne spoke of.

Here the author of the *Cloud* simply says: "All of mankind living on earth will be helped by this work in wonderful ways of which you are not even aware . . . And you yourself are cleansed and made virtuous by no other work as much as by this. And yet this is the simplest work of all, the easiest and the speediest to accomplish, if the soul is only helped by grace of feeling a strong desire to do it. Otherwise it is hard, and a marvel if you do it" (p. 62). "For this is a work . . . that man would have continued to do if he had never sinned. And it was for this work that man was made as all things also were made to help him and further him in this work, so that by means of it man shall be made whole again" (p. 65).

There is, in fact, in all the English mystics a characteristic realization of wholeness, of restoration, of return to a primitive state of innocence. The English mystics are Paradise men and the more clear and spontaneous their awareness of Paradise, the more truly English is their contemplation.

The author of the *Cloud* is perhaps, for some readers, the most difficult of them all to understand. He might seem to have nothing definite to say. He might seem to be maddeningly elusive. When you ask him precisely what the "work" is and how it is to be done, he says: "I don't know." For this is a way that cannot be understood by mental activity, it cannot be forced by an effort of the will. It is a pure response to the mysterious appeal of a hidden and incomprehensible God. It is a "wrestling with blind nought," and he is at great pains to contradict Augustine and to warn against thinking of it going on "inside" yourself or even "above" yourself. Where then is this work to be done? He answers, "Nowhere!"

JULIAN OF NORWICH

It is not so proper to speak of "Juliana" of Norwich as it is to call her by her true name, the "Lady Julian." Lady not because she was noble but because she was a *Domna,* like the Benedictine nuns of Carrow to whom her anchorhold at St. Julian's Church, Norwich, most probably belonged. Of all the English mystics, Julian of Norwich is perhaps the best known and the most charming. She is the English equivalent of Siena's Catherine and Sweden's Bridget, except that, unlike her great contemporaries, she did not concern herself with the problems of kingdoms and of the Church, but lived as a recluse in her quiet corner. Yet Norwich was not so far from the Continent that rumors of its wars and movements did not come through in plenty by way of the wool ports of the North Sea.

There can be no doubt that Lady Julian is the greatest of the English mystics. Not only that, but she is one of the greatest English theologians, in the ancient sense of the word. As Evagrius Ponticus said in the fourth century, "he who really prays is a theologian and he who is a theologian really prays." By prayer, of course, this Desert Father and Origenist meant the "theologia," which was at once contemplation and experience of the deepest revealed mysteries: the mystical knowledge of the Holy Trinity. Actually, in Julian of Norwich, we find an admirable synthesis of mystical experience and theological reflection, ranging from "bodily visions" of the passion of Christ to "intellectual visions" of the Trinity, and from reflections on the creation and providence to intuitions penetrating the inmost secret of the redemption and the divine mercy.

It would be insufficient and inexact to classify the teaching of Julian of Norwich merely as "private revelation." Certainly she did receive "Revelations of Divine Love" equal to those of St. Theresa of Avila or St. Margaret Mary, and that is the title of her book. These revelations, however, must be seen for what they are: as profound and penetrating supernatural experiences of the truths revealed to and taught by the Church. Furthermore, we must distinguish in Julian the record of the experiences themselves, the "sixteen shewings" which took place when she lay at death's door on May 13, 1383, and her subsequent reflections on these experiences, her elaboration of their meaning and of their import. It must be stressed that her whole book is completely objective. Though it is at the same time entirely personal, it cannot be regarded merely as an interesting account of subjective experiences. It is a document that bears eloquent witness to the teaching and tradition of the Catholic Church, and it is a meditative, indeed a mystical, commentary on the basic doctrines of the Catholic faith.

In a word, Julian of Norwich gives a coherent and indeed systematically constructed corpus of doctrine, which has only recently begun to be studied as it deserves.[13]

The theology of Lady Julian is a theol-

ogy of the all-embracing totality and fullness of the divine love. This is, for her, the
ultimate Reality, in the light of which all
created being and all the vicissitudes of life
and of history fade into unimportance.
Not that the world and time, the cosmos
and history are unreal: but their reality is
only a revelation of love. The revelation
itself is not immediately clear, however. A
gift of God is required before the light
breaks through and the full meaning of the
world and of time is seen in its real relation to God and to His eternal and loving
designs.

Julian "saw" the whole world as a "little thing the size of a hazel nut which
seemed to lie in the palm of my hand."
When she wondered what this was, "it
was answered in a general way, thus: 'it is
all that is made.' " And she adds: "I wondered how long it could last; for it seemed
as though it might suddenly fade away to

nothing, it was so small."[14] But the importance of this vision lies, paradoxically, in the fact that it shows not the *insignificance* of the created world so much as its *significance*. Though ontologically the being of the world is as nothing compared with the infinite God, yet it is willed and held in being by His love and is thus infinitely precious in His sight. For thus it becomes, itself, a revelation of His infinite love.

> It lasts and ever shall last for God loveth
> it. And even so hath everything being—
> by the love of God. In this little thing I
> saw three properties. The first that God
> made it: the second that God loveth it;
> the third that God keepeth it. And what
> beheld I in this? Truly the Maker, the
> Lover and the Keeper.[15]

Not only that, but in this same vision Julian sees herself, along with all beings, wrapped and embraced in the love of God so that: "He is to us everything that is good, as I understand it." And: "He is our clothing that, for love, wrapped us up and windeth us about; embraceth us, all be-clotheth us and hangeth about us, for tender love."[16]

The divine love manifested in creation is manifested more clearly and on a much deeper level in the Redemption. And here the originality of Julian lies, in her peculiar insight into the deeply personal and gratu-itous character of God's redemptive and merciful love. Here we see a new empha-sis, not on Christ's work of atonement, re-pairing the outraged justice of God the Fa-ther, but on the contrary, the redeemed sinner becomes the Father's merciful gift to the Son, "his bliss, his prize, his worship and his crown" (p. 83). The theology of Julian of Norwich is a theology of mercy, of joy, and of praise. Nowhere in all Christian literature are the dimensions of her Christian optimism excelled. Christ asks her if she is "well paid" that He suffered for her. It is a deep and illuminating question. Is she "satisfied" with the work He has done, is she "content" with Him? Is she so content that this alone suffices to content her? Is His love enough for her? She answers that it is. And He replies:

> If thou art paid, I am paid. It is a joy, a bliss and an endless liking to me that I ever suffered passion for thee. And if I could suffer more I would suffer more.[17]

This opens up new perspectives in the Augustinian tradition of *amor amicitiae,* disinterested love. Julian's vision of the divine mercy as a "motherly" love for us stems, perhaps, in part from St. Anselm. At any rate, she is not afraid to speak, with an utterly disarming simplicity, of "Jesus our

Mother." "Our Savior is our true Mother, in whom we are endlessly borne; and we shall never come out of Him" (p. 157). "God almighty is our kindly Father; and God allwisdom is our kindly Mother: with the love and goodness of the Holy Ghost; which is all one God, one Lord. And in the knitting and the oneing He is our very true Spouse, and we are His loved wife and fair maiden" (p. 158). "Our Father willeth, our Mother worketh, and our good Lord the Holy Ghost confirmeth" (p. 162).

It can be seen that Julian's mystical theology culminates in the vision and mystery of the Trinity and here there remain depths to be fathomed which we cannot pause to consider here. One last thought: we must emphasize the originality of Julian's intuition of the problem of evil in the light of the divine mercy. This is the subject of the great thirteenth revelation: "Sin must needs be, but all shall be well. All shall be well; and all manner of thing shall be well" (p. 91). We recall the echoes of this sentence in T. S. Eliot's *Four Quartets*.

Julian's vision of sin and mercy is remarkable above all for its realism. She minimizes nothing. She does not try to bolster up an optimistic explanation of redemption by minimizing sin. Such interpretations betray the mystery of the mercy of God revealed in the Gospel. She sees sin in all its tragedy, she sees the full horror and evil of the crucifixion of Christ. Not only that, she sees that sin persists and evil continues in the world. Indeed, it may grow, and there will come a time when "Holy Church shall be shaken with sorrow and anguish and tribulation in this world as men shake a cloth in the wind" (p. 92). She sees, moreover, the sufferings of the just and the crushing humiliations of those who strive to love Christ: their pain, their anguish, their descent into the abyss of near despair.

Here we come to what is perhaps the most personal and unique intuition in the revelations of Julian of Norwich. It is her distinction between the mystery of sin and redemption as proposed "openly" by the Church and Julian's conviction that this also implies "secretly" something that has never been revealed and which no one will know until the end of time. That though there is great evil in the world, though there are devils and a hell, with the damned in it, and though the Church shall be attacked and shaken in a great storm, yet the Lord assures her: "I *may* make all things well: and I *can* make all things well: and I *shall* make all things well and I *will* make all things well: and *thou shalt see thyself* that all manner of things shall be well" (p. 96). This is not a *solution* to the problem of evil. It is an admission that there exists no satisfactory intellectual solution. It is, even in spite of revelation, a problem that has not yet been fully solved and cannot be solved until the end of time when Christ Himself will make known something that has never been revealed before: the secret which He alone knows, and which it is not given us to know, which not even the blessed in heaven have yet seen, because it is not necessary for our salvation. It is the "secret counsel," the "great deed ordained by our Lord from without—beginning treasured and hid in His blessed breast, known only to Himself, by which He shall make all things well. For just as the blessed Trinity made all things from naught, so the same blessed Trinity shall make all well that is not well" (p. 99).

RECENT STUDIES

Both in Professor Knowles's study and in Professor Colledge's anthology we meet Margery Kempe. She is no equal to Julian, not because she was not a recluse (for she was married), but because she seems after all to have been a little hysterical, something of a garrulous busybody perhaps: at least, enough of one for Knowles to compare her, surprisingly, with Chaucer's Wife of Bath.

Margery was not quite as earthy as Chaucer's engaging character. But, still, she did not hesitate to tell her husband she felt she had married beneath her station, and decided to improve her financial condition by running a brewery, which unfortunately failed. Her business losses contributed something to her disillusionment with the world. Her life was certainly not without fantastic incidents. Once when she was hearing Mass a stone fell out of the church ceiling and hit her on the head. It bounced off "miraculously," without doing her any notable harm. She tells us it was on the road from York to Bridlington, while she was carrying a bottle of beer and her husband a cake, that she asked him if he would agree to their living thenceforth in chastity, and had her way. In return, she paid all his debts. She was nearly burned alive by a crowd in Canterbury. Doubtless, they imagined her to be a Lollard, because she preached to them against swearing and quoted abundantly from Scripture.

The mysticism of Margery Kempe is admittedly "original," if not strange. Once at the elevation of the Mass, she saw the Host "flutter like a dove" and took this as a prophetic intimation of a coming earthquake. No earthquake came.

She used to utter loud cries when in ecstasy. She believed herself mystically wedded, in a solemn rite, to the Heavenly Father. She heard the Holy Ghost singing like a robin.

It is not surprising that her orthodoxy was questioned, but an official examination acquitted her of heresy. Nevertheless, she was frequently imprisoned and even denounced from the pulpit, but she also had staunch friends and defenders among the clergy.

Today, E. I. Watkin has undertaken to write "In Defense of Margery Kempe."[18] While admitting that her behavior was odd, he stresses her subjective sincerity and her real virtue, especially her charity. What others have disapproved as "hysteria," Watkin prefers to call "abnormal suggestibility," and even admits that this suggestibility can be regarded at times as "morbid."

While not agreeing completely with Watkin's spirited defense of Margery, we can certainly recognize that it is a realistic estimate of a remarkably interesting figure seen in the context of her time. After all, the fourteenth century was an age of enthusiasm and of exaggeration.

Eric Colledge questions her mysticism more diffidently than Knowles, but both agree that, as a document of unrivaled historic interest, her autobiography is at once fascinating and invaluable.

Finally, there is Augustine Baker, who provides material for one of the most interesting and controversial articles in David Knowles's book. Born of a Protestant family in 16th-century Wales, Baker went to London to read for the bar and during his residence in the Inns of Court used to frequent the theaters, where he saw Shakespeare's new plays. He was converted, not indeed by Shakespeare but by a narrow escape from death, which he considered miraculous. He crossed over to the Continent, entered the Benedictine Order in Italy, but could not adjust to the systems of meditation and piety that were intensively practiced after the Council of Trent. Indeed, he thought they nearly drove him crazy, and when he later became a director of nuns in France, he dedicated all his efforts to rescuing potential contemplatives from the deadly machinery of systems which had their place in the active life but were less helpful in the cloister. He believed the monastic life ought naturally to lead one to "introversion." Never a community man, he led a marginal life as a semirecluse.

Knowles makes a careful study of this restless and complex character, this monastic oddball, born out of due season, in perpetual hopeless conflict with the "active-livers" in the cloister. He resisted them so doggedly that finally one of them, who came to be his superior, decided to get rid of him by sending him, in sickness and old age, to the English mission in a time of renewed persecution. Baker died in his bed, however, a "baffling figure," a "man of whimsies and corners," and, after all, we cannot help feeling that he was a creature of the fourteenth century who would have blossomed as happily as any Rolle or Lady Julian in an East Midland hermitage, but who had the misfortune to be born two centuries late. Since then, how many other such men have there been in England? We have mentioned William Blake: what would he have been in the fourteenth century? Perhaps the equal of Tauler, or Eckhart—or, more likely, Boehme. But nothing could stop Blake from being Blake. There is no century possible in which Blake would not have seen angels.

What is to be said of Knowles's treatment of the English mystics? It is an excellent, interesting, and well-written book, but its judgments are too rigid and too strict. It suffers from a kind of scholarly compulsion to deny and to reject, as if the most important task of the student of mysticism were to uncover false mystics. Indeed, Knowles is so cautious that, out of six "mystics," he ends up by accepting only three as fully genuine. Margery Kempe, of course, he dismissed as "sincere, devout, but very hysterical," after a consideration of her vision of "many white things flying all about her on every side as thick as motes in a sunbeam." After a patient examination of Baker, Professor Knowles concludes that he never developed into "a genuine mystic." This judgment has been vigorously and I believe rightly disputed by E. I. Watkin. There will certainly be few to accept without question Knowles's minimizing of Richard Rolle as a "beginner."

Knowles clings firmly to a single standard in judging mystics: it is the Dionysian standard of "unknowing." Therefore, he cannot accept as genuine a mystic of light like Rolle. The "fire, song and sweetness" of the hermit of Hampole are, by Knowles's standards, merely the consolations that precede and prepare for the serious business of dark contemplation.

But is it, after all, realistic to cling arbitrarily to a single set standard in such a thing as mysticism, in which the great rule is that there are no rules? The Holy Ghost takes temperaments as He finds them and does what He pleases with them. The history of mysticism, including patristic mysticism, gives us plenty of room for accepting the "fire of love" in Rolle as something more than "sensible consolation." After all, does not Cassian speak of the "prayer of fire" among the Desert Fathers? (Admittedly, this is an illumination that pertains more to *theoria physike* than to perfect mysticism.) But, more serious than this, to reject a mysticism like Rolle's would mean rejecting the mysticism of the Oriental Church.

As a matter of fact, Rolle resembles the Hesychast mystics of Sinai and Mount Athos in more than one point. Not only does he experience the presence of the glorified Saviour in a flood of light, but his ordinary prayer, besides the Psalter, is the meditative and loving repetition of the Name of Jesus. More exactly, it is a constant mindfulness of the Holy Name present as a living and sanctifying power in the depths of the heart. *"Ponder [this Name of Jesus] in thy heart night and day as a special and dear treasure. Love it more than thy life, root it in thy mind . . ."* (R. Rolle, *The Commandment*).

Here we have a close parallel to the famous "Prayer of Jesus" propagated not only in monastic but also in lay circles throughout Greece and Russia by the *Philokalia.*

A study of the controversy between Barlaam the Calabrian and Gregory Palamas will warn us not to be too adamant in clinging to the apophatic standard in mysticism. Indeed, *apophasis* (the mysticism of darkness) and *cataphasis* (the mysticism of light) are simply correlative to one another, and Pseudo-Denys makes clear that "mystical theology" rises above both of them and completes them both in a darkness that is "superresplendent." The "light of Tabor," which is at the heart of Athonite mysticism, surely seems to bear witness in favor of Rolle, and when we read about Seraphim of Sarov visibly transfigured by the in-dwelling Spirit, we must hesitate to dismiss this prayer of fire without any other reason than that it does not correspond with the standards of the *Cloud of Unknowing*. After all, according to St. John of the Cross, to whom Knowles turns as a court of last appeal, it could be argued that the author of the *Cloud* was simply a "beginner" in dark contemplation.

A more moderate judgment of Rolle is that of Father Conrad Pepler, O.P., who admits there is no doubt of the genuine mystical character of Rolle's experience. It is an "infused" and "mystical" gift, granted to an "exceptionally devoted man" who had lived a heroically ascetic life. But, says Father Pepler, "his life and teaching are characteristic of the illuminative way rather than of the supreme heights."[19] This fits in with the language of St. John of the Cross, who, in the *Spiritual Canticle*, describes relatively advanced mystical states as "the illuminative way," reserving the term "unitive way" for that transforming union which presupposes the rare and intense purification brought about by the dark night of the spirit. And there is no evidence of this dark night in Rolle. One finds in him perhaps too much passion, too much poetry, too much of an active "self" who rises to the occasion and justifies his mystical love in the flames not only of ecstasy but of controversy. Not a few saints have done the same: so who are we to weigh and measure and, with extreme exactitude, to mark out degrees? Too much nicety, and too many preoccupations in judging the mystics make it impossible for us to enter, by empathy, into a valid appreciation of their experience, and thus we can no longer really judge it.

To reject Rolle as an undeveloped mystic is, finally, to reject that which seems distinctly characteristic of the northern English solitaries, as exemplified by the twelfth-century hermit, poet, and predecessor of Rolle, Godric of Finchale, in whose heart "there was a gentleness greater than anything else, in his mouth a sweetness sweeter than honey or the honeycomb and his ears were filled with the melody of a great jubilation." These words of a medieval hagiographer are borrowed from a sermon of St. Bernard, yet they serve to express a characteristic type of mystical experience. However much we may ourselves prefer the mystics of darkness, we cannot hastily reject the mysticism of light.

Though this is no slight criticism, it does not alter our admiration for Knowles's book or for its author. This is a work of singular excellence. No one who loves the English spiritual tradition can read it without passionate interest and deep concern.

CONCLUSIONS

This brief introduction will have given us a good idea of the main characteristics of English mysticism. When we consider the fourteenth-century "school" of English mysticism, we find in it first of all a certain coherence and unity of temper, even though there may be wide differences between the individual mystics. This coherence is due perhaps above all to the fact that it is a small school, in an island nation. Influences from abroad undoubtedly arrive and lead some of them into new directions. This is probably particularly true of the *Cloud of Unknowing,* which we may perhaps owe to a current of Dionysian spirituality from the Rhineland. Yet it is not absolutely necessary to account for the *Cloud* by tracing it to Eckhart and Tauler. There was after all the school of St. Victor in Paris, with Richard of St. Victor, a Scot and one of the medieval theorists of dark contemplation, who was widely read in England. But we are not here preoccupied with influences, since whatever they may have been, these influences were absorbed

into peculiarly English minds and doctrines.

Whether they are mystics of darkness
or of light, the masters of the English
school are all equally positive, optimistic,
simple. The author of the *Cloud* talks of
"darkness" and "nothing" and yet he does
not strike us as much less luminous than
Rolle with his "fire, song and sweetness."
The mysticism of darkness is not a mysticism of gloom. We must remember how
these mystics appropriated the verse of the
psalm, *Nox illuminatio mea in deliciis meis*
(Night is my light in my delights). It is
a darkness illuminated by joy and by the
presence of the Lord, all the more joyous
precisely because the night brings Him
nearer and unites us to Him more inti-
mately than any light.

The masters of the English school, each
in his own way, teach a doctrine of simplicity and joy. One finds in them nothing

tragic, nothing morbid, no obsession, no violence. Of course, one must make an exception for Margery Kempe. She was odd and she made a lot of noise, but nobody took this seriously or encouraged her to do so. There is in the English school less blood and anguish, less hellfire and horror, than is to be found in any other school of Christian mysticism. Not that the physical sufferings of Christ on the cross were not real to them, witness the first shewing of Lady Julian: but the light of mercy and the joy of life in the Risen Saviour transfigure even the vision of the Crucified. And this is, of course, as it should be.

English mysticism is, then, always positive, always affirmative, even when, like the *Cloud,* it negates. For what is negated is the accidental, the relative, the inconsequential, in order that first things may be put first, and the great, eternal truths affirmed. One finds relatively little of the devil in English mysticism: not that he is ignored, but the English mystics were more impressed with the power of Christ than with the power of Satan.

English mysticism is a mysticism of praise, and consequently it tends to take an affirmative view of God's creation and of human existence in the world. Not that it is what men now call a "world-affirm-ing" spirituality, concerned with establish-ing the Kingdom of God in a solid political and economic setting. It is rather a "para-dise spirituality" which recovers in Christ the innocence and joy of the first begin-nings and sees the world—the lovely world of moors and wolds, midland for-ests, rivers and farms—in the light of Par-adise, as it first came from the hand of God. Even the author of the *Cloud,* who is less disposed than the others to "see" these things, does not ignore them.

As people, the English mystics are al-

ways very human, and, we may add, very
individual. One might perhaps even be
tempted to call them "individualists," but
that word has overtones that would not be
true in the case of men and women who
in no way lived for themselves or centered
on themselves. The English mystics were
certainly aware of themselves as autono-
mous persons loved and redeemed by God.
They attached great importance to this
fact, and they recognized it with great
simplicity, dignity, and gratitude. They
recognized their personal vocation as a gift
of wonderful meaning and value. They
sought above all to be faithful to the grace
of their calling. They took the gift of contemplation seriously, and were not too
concerned with the possible approval or
disapproval of other men. One senses in
them a fine respect for individual differences in these matters. Sometimes this re-

spect was bought and defended with a great price.

Finally, it can be said without exaggeration that the chief characteristic of the English school of the fourteenth century, its homogeneous, simple, optimistic, and personal quality, is perhaps due above all to the fact that it developed out of the English monastic tradition. The mysticism of the English school is basically Benedictine and Cistercian. This does not mean to say, as Dom Cuthbert Butler once held, that it is purely and simply a "genuine Western mysticism" rooted in Augustine and not in the writings of that dubious Oriental, the Pseudo-Areopagite. It means, on the contrary, that it goes back to the same root as Pseudo-Denys: through Cassian and Gregory the Great to Evagrius Ponticus, the Desert Fathers, and Origen. Of course, Augustine has a great deal to say in and through the English mystics. His Trinitarian psychology is there, the doctrine of image and likeness is there, and the introversion by which we enter into ourselves and then go on above ourselves is also there. True, also, the *Cloud* goes direct to Pseudo-Dionysius and makes a special point of attacking the Augustinian psychology of contemplation. But these varieties were already present within the monastic tradition itself. It may be argued that the English mystics were, for the most part, either solitaries or oriented toward the eremitical life. This does nothing to disprove that their mysticism is rooted in the medieval monastic tradition of England, since the English hermits were, obviously, the full flower of the monastic tradition. Yet, at the same time, the hermit had been from the beginning more a "layman" than a "clerk." That is to say, even if he may have been a priest, his separation from the monastic and liturgical community life put him in a certain sense on a level with the simple layman. The hermit life, properly understood, is a life without exaltation, a life not at the top of the ladder but in a certain sense at the bottom. For more than anyone else the hermit has to be a humble man. This combination of simplicity, individuality, and humility, not without ever present elements of humor, is proper to a spirituality of men and women who have gone apart to live alone with God.

RUSSIAN MYSTICS

RUSSIAN MYSTICISM is predominantly monastic (though one meets an occasional exception like the modern non-monastic mystics, Father John of Kronstadt—recently canonized by the Orthodox Church—and Father Yelchaninov). It therefore thrives in solitude and renunciation of the world. Yet anyone who has even the most superficial acquaintance with Russian Christendom is aware that the monasteries of Russia, even more than those of the West, exercised a crucially important influence on society, whether as centers of spiritual life and transformation to which pilgrims flocked from everywhere, or as bases for missionary expansion, or, finally, as powerful social forces sometimes manipulated—or suppressed —for political advantage. Such struggles as those between St. Nilus of Sora and St. Joseph of Volokolamsk speak eloquently of the age-old conflict, within monasticism itself, between the charismatic drive to solitary contemplation plus charismatic pastoral action, and the institutional need to fit the monastic community into a structure of organized socio-religious power, as a center of liturgy and education and as a nursery of bishops.

Other conflicts, such as that between Eastern Orthodox spirituality and Westernizing influences, play an important part in the lives of the monks and mystics of Russia. Many students of Russian spirituality will be surprised to learn what a great part Western theological attitudes and devotions played in the formation of St. Tikhon in the eighteenth century. The seminary which Tikhon attended was organized on the Jesuit pattern and yet he was not influenced by post-Tridentine Catholic thought. Dr. Bolshakoff identifies him rather with German pietism. In any case, we must not be too quick to assume that St. Tikhon's spirituality is purely and ideally "Russian." Yet, paradoxically, this combination of Western and Eastern holiness is a peculiarly Russian phenomenon. St. Tikhon was perhaps the greatest mystic of the age of rationalist enlightenment.

Russian mysticism is to be traced largely to the greatest monastic center of Orthodox mysticism, Mount Athos. Ever since the eleventh century the Russian monastic movement had been nourished by direct contact with the "Holy Mountain"—interrupted only by the Tatar invasions of the Middle Ages. Liturgy, asceticism, and mysticism in Russia owed their development in great part not to literary documents but to the living experience of pilgrim monks who spent a certain time at Athos, either in the "Rossikon" (the Russian monastery of St. Panteleimon) or in various sketes and cells, before returning to found new monasteries or renew the life of old ones in their country. Periods when, for one reason or another, communication with Athos has diminished have also been periods of monastic decline in Russia.

One of the characteristic fruits of Russian monachism on Athos is the "Prayer of Jesus," the constant repetition of a short formula in conjunction with rhythmic breathing and with deep faith in the supernatural power of the Holy Name. This was a Russian development of the Greek Hesychast way of prayer taught by St. Gregory Palamas. The "Prayer of Jesus" became the normal way of contemplative prayer in Russian monasticism, but, more important still, it was adopted on all sides by devout lay people, especially among the masses of the poor peasantry.

Until recently, Western theologians were highly suspicious of Athonite "Hesychasm" and regarded it as perilous, even heretical. Deeper study and a wider acquaintance with non-Western forms of spirituality have made Hesychasm seem a little less outlandish. It is now no longer necessary to repeat the outraged platitudes of those who thought that the Hesychasts were practicing self-hypnosis, or who believed that, at best, the monks of Athos were engaged in a kind of Western Yoga.

The "Prayer of Jesus," made known to Western readers by the "Tale of the Pilgrim," surely one of the great classics of the literature of prayer, is now practiced not only by characters in Salinger's novels but even at times by some Western monks. Needless to say, a way of prayer for which, in its land of origin, the direction of a "starets" was mandatory, is not safely to be followed by us in the West without professional direction.

The mystical Russian "pilgrim" received from his starets an anthology of patristic quotations on prayer: the famous *Philokalia*. The monastic reformer, Paisius Velichkovsky (1722–94), after living for some time in a skete on Mount Athos during a period of monastic decline, translated the *Philokalia* into Slavonic and introduced it to Russia. It was then done into Russian by another mystic, Bishop Theophane the Recluse.

Paisius and his disciples also translated other works of the Fathers and in addition to this exercised a direct and living influence on Russian monachism through the numerous pilgrims who constantly visited in monasteries reformed by him in Moldavia and Walachia. Here visitors from all parts of Russia encountered not only a pure and austere monastic discipline but also the spiritual direction of specialists in asceticism and Hesychast prayer, who came to be known as *startsy*. The translations of the *Philokalia*, the monastic reform of Paisius, and especially *Starchestvo*, the direction of the startsy, set in motion the great development that was to make the nineteenth century the golden age of Russian mysticism. This was also the time when the Rossikon on Mount Athos reached its peak in numbers, fervor, and prosperity.

One of the best-known (or least-unknown) of the Russian mystics is St. Seraphim of Sarov, who lived the life of a Desert Father in the forests at the beginning of the nineteenth century. He affords a striking contrast to other post-medieval saints and ascetics who have tried to imitate the Desert Fathers. In many of these, together with a sincere ascetic and monastic purpose and devotion to authentic ideals, we seem to encounter a spirit of willfulness that is often violent and artificial even to the point of obsession. As a result, we find a negative, gloomy, and tense spirituality in which one is not sure whether the dominant note is hatred of wickedness or love of good—and hatred of wickedness can so easily include hatred of human beings, who are perhaps less wicked than they seem. The study of ascetic tradition and the passion for austerity do not suffice by themselves to make monastic saints, although it must be admitted that a specious "humanism" which turns its back on all austerity and solitude is hardly more effective in this regard!

Whether or not Seraphim had studied ancient monastic tradition, it is certain that he was a living and spontaneous exemplar of the most authentic monastic ideal. His solitary life in the forest was extremely austere and yet his spirituality was marked by pure joy. Though he gave himself unsparingly to each ascetic exploit (*podvig*), he remained simple, childlike, meek, astonishingly open to life and to other men, gentle, and profoundly compassionate.

He is without doubt the greatest mystic of the Russian Church, and the Hesychast tradition is evident in his mysticism of light. Yet Hesychasm is, so to speak, absorbed in the Evangelical and patristic purity of his experience of the great Christian mystery, the presence of the Spirit given by God through the Risen Christ to His Body, the Church.

Seraphim's simplicity reminds us in many ways of Francis of Assisi, though his life was more like that of Anthony of the Desert. But like every other great contemplative saint, Seraphim had his eyes wide open to the truth of the Gospel, and could not understand how the rest of men could be content with an "enlightenment" that was in reality nothing but ignorance and spiritual blindness. The only contemporary figure in the West who speaks so eloquently and with such ingenuous amazement of the divine light shining in darkness is the English poet William Blake. But there is in Seraphim none of Blake's gnosticism: only the pure and traditional theology of the Church.

Seraphim of Sarov is then the most perfect example of that mysticism of light which is characteristic of the Orthodox Church: completely positive and yet compatible with, indeed based on, the apophatic (negative) theology of Pseudo-Dionysius and St. Maximus the Confessor. It is perhaps this which distinguishes Russian mysticism in its pure state. Not an intellectualist and negative ascent to the Invisible above all that is visible, but more paradoxically an apprehension of the invisible as visible insofar as all creation is suddenly experienced as transfigured in a light for which there is no accounting in terms of any philosophy, a light which is given directly by God, proceeds from God, and in a sense *is* the Divine Light. Yet this experience is not a substantial vision of God, because in Oriental theology the light experienced by the mystic is a divine "energy," distinct from God's nature but which can be apprehended in contact with the *Person* of the Holy Spirit, by mystical love and grace.

Thus, it is easy to see that though there are in Russia some instances of a negative mysticism comparable to the Dark Night in St. John of the Cross, yet they are not characteristic of Russian mystical theology, which is a theology not of suffering but of transfiguration.

Nevertheless, this theology of resurrection and joy is firmly based on repentance and on tears, and one does not easily find in it the impertinences of a devout sentimentality which simply assumes that "everything is bound to turn out all right." The reality of redemption and transfiguration depends on the most basic experience of the evil of sin.

Not all the Russian mystics were able to experience this evil as totally consumed in the flames of Redemptive Love. Bishop Ignatius Brianchaninov, an aristocrat and an army engineer converted to the monastic life, looked out upon the world with profound pessimism. The world of matter was not, for him, transfigured by the divine light: it was purely and simply the subject of corruption. For him (as for so many others in the nineteenth century), science and religion were in conflict, and to know Christ one had to reject all earthly knowledge as false and totally misleading. And yet science does nevertheless contribute something of positive value to the meditations of Bishop Brianchaninov. However, we observe with regret in Brianchaninov a tendency to impose a kind of unnatural constraint upon the body and the mind, and we are not surprised when he informs us that he considers visions of devils rather a usual thing in the monastic life. His pessimism and suspicion toward women as such blend with the rest of his dark view of things. Yet, even where his negative attitude repels us, we must admit he often displays remarkable psychological insight. All in all, Brianchaninov is too rigid, too suspicious of the light, too closed to ordinary human experience to impress us as St. Seraphim does. And yet it would seem that the negativism of Brianchaninov had a deeper influence on nineteenth-century Russian monasticism than the marvelous Gospel optimism of St. Seraphim. The works of Brianchaninov will help us to understand the conservative reaction of Leontiev and of the monks of Optino against Dostoevsky's idealized and forward-looking portrait of Starets Zosima.

This portrait was supposed to have been based on the living figure of Starets Ambrose of Optino, but the monks in general rejected its optimism, its "humanism," as untrue to the genuine monastic tradition of Russia. Perhaps the generality of monks were more disposed to look at life through the embittered and blazing eyes of the fanatical ascetic Ferrapont, in whom Dostoevsky himself evidently intended to portray the kind of negativism typified by the old school, and critics and opponents of the startsy.

It is curious that the Russian revolution was preceded not by a century of monastic decadence and torpor, but by a monastic Golden Age. But if the term "Golden Age" is to mean anything, it must mean a time of vitality. Vitality means variety, and this, in turn, may imply conflict. In nineteenth-century Russian monasticism we find darkness and light, world-denial and loving affirmation of human values, a general hardening of resistance to forces of atheist humanism and revolution, and yet an anguished concern at the sinful oppression of the poor. We cannot with justice dismiss the whole Russian monastic movement as negative, pessimistic, world-hating. Nor can we identify its deep and traditional contemplative aspirations with mere political or cultural conservatism. There was an unquestionably prophetic spirit at work in the movement, and St. Seraphim is only one among many examples that prove this. There was also a profound concern for "the world" and for humanity, a wonderful, unequaled compassion that reached out to all mankind and indeed to all living creatures, to embrace them in God's love and in merciful concern. It cannot be doubted that the great startsy, in their humane and tender simplicity, were sometimes completely identified with the humble and the poor. It would be ludicrous to class them as obscurantists and reactionaries.

On the other hand, there was a less prophetic, but nonetheless amazing spirit of ascetic fervor, of discipline, of order, which while it was undeniably one of the things that made the age "Golden," still had rather more human and even political implications. And here monasticism was, indeed, more deeply involved in social structures and national aspirations, even where it most forcefully asserted its hatred of "the world." Here, too, contempt for the world and pessimistic rigorism were in fact inseparable from social and political conservatism. The ascetic who renounced the city of man in order to lament his sins in the *poustyna* (desert) may well have been giving his support to a condition of social inertia by implicitly affirming that all concern with improvement was futile and even sinful. We may cite as an example Constantin Leontiev, Dostoevsky's adversary and critic, who entered a monastery, gloried in extreme austerity, and doubtless expressed monastic views that were those of most monks of the time.

Leontiev actually stated that the Orthodoxy on Mount Athos depended on the peace of the harmonious interaction of Turkish political power, Russian wealth, and Greek ecclesiastical authority. Most of his compatriots, monks included, were probably too nationalistic to follow this "realist" view all the way.[1] They were Pan-Slavist and therefore anti-Greek as well as anti-Western. But the point is that their monastic fervor formed part of a complex

Russian nationalist mystique and contributed much energy to it. The average good
monk, who was not raised by sanctity
above this level, tended to identify himself
and his religious ideal with this mystique
of Holy Russia. It would be very interesting to compare this with the ideas of such
lay theologians as Soloviev, who was very
open to Rome and the West, but space
does not permit here.

The doctrine of the Russian startsy of
the last hundred and fifty years is rich in
monastic wisdom, as well as in ordinary
religious psychology and plain good sense.
It is interesting to see that they were concerned with many traditional monastic
problems which are being rather warmly
discussed in Western monasteries today.
The answers to the startsy can be of special value to Western monks who are interested in discovering the deepest mean-

ing of their monastic vocation, and ways to live that vocation more perfectly.

The reason for this is perhaps simpler than one might expect. It is not so much that the startsy were exceptionally austere men, or that they had acquired great learning, but that they had surrendered themselves completely to the demands of the Gospel and to Evangelical charity, totally forgetting themselves in obedience to the Spirit of God so that they lived as perfect Christians, notable above all for their humility, their meekness, their openness to all men, their apparently inexhaustible capacity for patient and compassionate love. The purpose of *Starchestvo* is, then, not so much to make use of daily spiritual direction in order to inculcate a special method of prayer, but rather to keep the heart of the disciple open to love, to prevent it from hardening in self-centered concern (whether moral, spiritual, or ascetical). All the worst sins are denials and rejections of love, refusals to love. The chief aim of the starets is first to teach his disciple not to sin against love, then to encourage and assist his growth in love until he becomes a saint. This total surrender to the power of love was the sole basis of their spiritual authority, and on this basis the startsy demanded complete and unquestioning obedience. They could do so because they themselves never resisted the claims and demands of charity.

One cannot refrain from observing, in this connection, how much Pope John XXIII displayed this same charismatic and Evangelical openness. His life as Pope is filled with incidents in which this great warmhearted man unquestioningly obeyed the spirit of goodness that was in him, and met with consternation when he expected others to obey the same spirit with equal readiness! So many Christians exalt the demands and rigors of law because, in reality, law is less demanding than pure charity. The law, after all, has reasonable safe limits! One always knows what to expect, and one can always hope to evade, by careful planning, the more unpleasant demands!

The mention of Pope John naturally suggests a conclusion to this brief article. Pope John's love for the Church of the Orient, of Greece and Russia, is well known. His idea of calling the Second Vatican Council was prompted in large part by this love of our separated Orthodox brothers. Knowledge of the spirit and teaching of the Russian mystics can be of great help to us in carrying on the work of reunion which Pope John has bequeathed to us.

PROTESTANT
MONASTICISM

IT IS NO EXAGGERATION to say that
Protestantism was in part a result of the
monastic crisis of the late Middle Ages.
Luther's most characteristic theological
doctrines were shaped by his revolt against
the limitations of religious life in a community that was, if not totally corrupt, at
least subject to serious deficiencies. Sterile
devotionalism, attachment to trivial outward forms, forgetfulness of the essentials
of the Christian faith, and obsession with
accidentals drove Luther to a desperation
which may or may not have bordered on
the pathological. (It would seem that scru-
tiny of Luther's psychic condition has been

overdone!) In any case, these ills accounted to some extent for Luther's emphasis on *sola fides*. The "works" by which he denied that man could be justified were first of all the monastic observances which traditional Catholic theology had associated with the state of perfection, the life of the vows.

If Calvin and Luther had confined themselves to a theoretical dispute on justification, there might have been some hope of adjustment and reconciliation. In actual fact, the doctrine of justification by faith declared, as a practical corollary, that religious vows were not only reprehensible but invalid. It emptied the convents and monasteries of Germany. From that time on, one might assume that "Protestantism" and "monasticism" were mutually exclusive and that such a thing as "Protestant monasticism" was inconceivable. (It

must, of course, be remembered that Anglican monasticism is not "Protestant.")

Yet, since Taizé has found space in the
popular press, everyone is aware of the
very significant Protestant monastic revival
going on today. As a matter of fact, it is
perhaps in Protestantism that the more
general monastic movement has gathered
the strongest momentum and displayed
the greatest vitality in the shortest time.
One might even hazard the opinion that
these Protestant communities are the most
telling and hopeful signs of life in the monastic revival today.

There has evidently been a crucially important shift in Protestant perspective. No
longer is it universally taken for granted
that the monastic way is a purely man-
made invention superimposed upon the
Gospel of Christ, and diverting attention
from the true message of salvation. No
longer are vows regarded by all Protes-

tants as useless constraints, mortgaging the future and binding the religious to sterile trivialities instead of fruitful and spontaneous Christian action. Most important of all, Protestant monasticism implies a rediscovery of the contemplative patterns of life characteristic of the ancient Catholic orders. Active works of charity have an important place in the life of the new communities, but it may be said that they are predominantly contemplative. Contemplation and prayer are by no means considered "idleness."

These communities, however, are not committed to *a priori* formulations, Roger Schutz, founder and prior of Taizé, has said: "Experience of the needs of our times and the meditation in common of the Gospels led the brothers to give definite form to their original vocation"—a form, however, which is not yet so definite as to preclude spontaneous development in the future.

The life of vows, under a rule, must not be allowed to sterilize the liberty and spontaneity which they are meant to consecrate to God. "The Rule [of Taizé] must never be regarded as an end in itself or dispense us from ever more seeking to discover God's design, the love of Christ and the light of the Holy Spirit." The original intuitions of the Reformation have not been abandoned. Taizé believes that a rule that surreptitiously took the place of the Gospel would be nothing but a "useless burden."

One of the special qualities of these Protestant communities is their freedom, their flexibility in meeting crucial needs of our time, not in stereotyped institutional ways (schools, clubs, etc.), but with an apostolic spontaneity nourished by monasticity of life.

Father Biot, a Dominican, has written a concise, sympathetic, and very welcome study of this paradoxical new movement.[1] The recently founded communities of France, Germany, and Switzerland are mentioned, briefly described, and placed in their historical setting. The author is, however, not interested in a journalistic presentation of his subject, or in a monastic travelogue. He is chiefly concerned with a theological explanation of the monastic movement in Protestantism, and he sees it *in a general context of theological awakening,* Protestant, Catholic, and Orthodox. It is another aspect of the Christian renewal which is manifest in the Liturgical, Biblical, and Ecumenical movements.

Father Biot demonstrates, first of all, that the sixteenth-century reformers did not absolutely exclude a dedicated life. The possibility of a special vocation and of vows was generally conceded. The renunciation practiced by the third-century ascetes and the early monks was sometimes admitted as having had value. The decision against vows was made in a definite historical context, in which the Reformers saw the vows violated on every side. They were convinced that modern men and women could not meet the obligation of lifelong chastity. But vows were not always regarded as intrinsically impossible or unChristian. A life of renunciation remained theoretically possible, even though impractical.

Though Karl Barth has always defended the classic doctrines of the Reformation and is therefore not inclined to overestimate the value of asceticism as a way of Christian perfection, he still recognizes a vocation to celibacy, and esteems monasticism insofar as it seems to him to have been, historically, a protest against the secularization of the Church. Barth approves the call to special renunciation and to liberty in Christ which monasticism issues to Christians in the world, and he asks, "Is there not a need to establish a pattern in which the place of the solitary life will always be assured?" It is precisely the notes of community in solitude, renunciation, and prayer that interest Protestant theologians of monasticism today.

The Protestant monastic movement is, then, much more than a pietistic diversion for a few enthusiasts, a quixotic imitation of Catholic observance. It is just as much a sign of true life and of Christian renewal as the other movements that have come into such prominence in the era of the Johannine Council. This is made evident by the close association of Protestant monasticism with liturgy, the Bible, and ecumenism, as well as by the authenticity of the monastic life that is being led in the new communities.

Protestant monasticism is not interested in merely *imitating* Catholic communities, but in discreetly helping and encouraging monastic reform wherever it is needed and possible. This implies no specific criticism of any set form of monasticism. But Taizé does offer a model of simplicity, spontaneity, openness, and vitality which can be profitably considered by the Catholic orders that have, perhaps in the course of centuries, become a little rigid. Above all, the Protestant communities can help Catholic monasticism to preserve its own authentic sense of values. There is a real danger of confusion in our own monastic communities, where a sense of uneasiness and insecurity often seeks to pacify itself by expedients that threaten to alienate us from our own inner truth. The fidelity of the new Protestant communities to genuine monastic values should reassure us, and encourage us to cling fearlessly to the ideal of solitude, prayer, renunciation, poverty, and work that ought to be ours.

Again, it is Prior Roger Schutz who tells us: "The reformation which ought to have taken place on the inside of the Catholic Church can penetrate it via the medium of charity, and succeed not by demolishing it but by causing those within it to recenter their attention on the essential treasures which it has always possessed."

The monastic life is one of those essential treasures. There is certainly great significance in the lesson which is being taught us by an apparently ironic Providence: that the Reformation which began by demolishing a whole segment of a tottering monastic fabric should now be seeking to help us rebuild it according to its primitive lines. This is a fact of capital importance in present-day ecumenism, and we can be grateful to Father Biot for making it clear. His book offers great encouragement to a monastic and ecumenical dialogue which has been going on for several years and is growing in importance and interest all the time.

PLEASANT HILL

A Shaker Village in Kentucky[1]

T HE SHAKERS, or rather "The United Society of Believers in Christ's Second Appearing," were most active in New England and upper New York State in the first half of the nineteenth century. They have almost completely died out today. At the time of their greatest expansion, they reached westward and established communities in Ohio, Indiana, and Kentucky. The simple, spacious buildings of the Kentucky Shaker colonies still stand: some of those at South Union were for a time occupied by the Benedictine Priory of St. Maur's. Those at Pleasant Hill, popularly known as "Shakertown," near Lexington, are being restored as a public monument.

As their official title suggests, the "Believers in Christ's Second Appearing" were people who had entirely forsaken secular society to set up a religious and prophetic commune, believing in the imminent end of the world. With them, as perhaps with some of the early monks, celibacy was held to be symbolic of the futility of generating any more human beings in a world ready for destruction and for renewal on an angelic plane. The term "Shakers" is due not only to the dancing and ecstatic experiences which marked their common worship, but perhaps especially to their belief that when the Holy Spirit was present He made Himself known by "shaking" the whole community in a kind of prophetic earthquake. The eschatological charity of the order produced an inward power which, they believed, would "shake" the world and prepare it for the millennial renewal.

The extraordinary theology of the Shakers, with its emphasis on the "Second Appearing" of Christ in a Woman, is only fully to be understood when we recognize its spiritual affinity with Gnosticism and Montanism. Yet there is a great independence and originality in the Shaker spirit. The "Woman," the embodiment of divine Wisdom in the last days of the world, and Daughter of the Holy Spirit, was Mother Ann Lee, who came to America from England with eight companions and landed in New York on the sixth of August, 1774. After gathering a small community at Watervliet, New York, in 1776, she laid the definitive foundations of her society at New Lebanon in 1779.

For many reasons, "ordinary" Americans of those revolutionary times found the Shakers disturbing, and subjected them to persecution. In the first place, the Shakers were pacifists. They refused to participate in the Revolutionary War on either side, which meant that they were considered "agents of the British" by patriotic Americans. Their fervent love of celibacy was closely connected with pacifism, for they held that lust and cruelty went together, and that unchastity led to avarice and attachment to worldly goods, which were protected or acquired by force. "Marriage," they declared, "is not a Christian institution, because the community of goods cannot be maintained therein . . . Wars are the results of lusts for lands and women. *Those who marry will fight.*"

The Shakers, being fully determined to do neither of these things, lived in peaceful, cenobitic communes, in which the sexes were kept firmly apart. In each "Family House," the men had their common dwelling on one side, the women on the other, and they used separate stairways to reach their isolated dormitories. In the last analysis, the real significance of their celibacy was their belief that they had been completely regenerated and were living the perfect risen life in and with Christ. "We have actually risen with Christ and travel with Him to the resurrection [i.e., of all flesh]," said one of the first Elders. But this rebirth to the angelic life could only be achieved by embracing perfect chastity, without which one could not be a genuine Christian. We can detect echoes of Catharism and Montanism, which, like the religion of the Shakers, placed a great emphasis on virginity and prophetic inspiration and attacked institutional religion. Like the Albigenses, the Shakers believed that the conventional organized "churches" had been reduced, by continual compromises, to complicity with the world in its lusts, its greed for money, and its appetite for power.

They felt that this was amply demon-

strated by the social injustices and inequal-
ities which were not only tolerated by
most Christians but actively encouraged
by them. Therefore, they concluded that
the Kingdom of God had not yet been established on earth since the professed fol-
lowers of Christ were obviously not imitating Him. A Shaker of the Harvard
Community wrote in 1853:

> [Jesus] was no speculator in stocks,
> trades, or estates. He could not be dis-
> tinguished by the carriage He rode in or
> the palace He dwelt in, nor the cloth He
> wore, by the multitude of His servants,
> golden ornaments, nor refined lit-
> erature . . .

Jesus was a simple carpenter, the apostles
were working men, Mother Ann and the
early Shakers were all simple working-class
people. The Shaker communities lived an

austere and disciplined life of renunciation and labor and it was their hard work that eventually won them the respect of their neighbors. Yet at the same time they were shrewd and practical in their dealings with the wicked world, and they sent their most businesslike representatives to market to buy and sell, so that even Emerson remarked caustically on their ability to drive a hard bargain.

We cannot safely judge the Shakers by what was said about them, especially in the beginning. They were accused by their enemies of everything from nudism and debauchery to being "the principal enemies of America." They are famous for the dancing which characterized their worship, and this dancing was a source of grave scandal to other Protestants, who felt that such "bodily agitation" was distinctly "Catholic." In fact, though the Shakers themselves believed that the

Church of Rome was the Great Whore of Babylon, along with all the other established institutional forms of Christianity, they themselves were considered to be "Papish" because public general confession of past sins was a prerequisite to admission, and after one was in the Society he had to obey the Ministers in perfect simplicity—a "Romish" practice.

In actual fact, their written records, their simple songs, and especially their "concentrated labor" show these believers to have been sincere, honest, modest people, minding their own business, devoted to their faith in the Second Coming of Christ, living already in another world in which they felt themselves close to the angels and to the Lord of angels, along with Mother Ann, who would soon usher them into the New Creation, the definitive Kingdom.

The most eloquent witness to the

Shaker spirit is the fruit of their labor. Anyone who knows anything about furniture realizes that today a mere stool, a coat hanger, a simple box made by the Shakers, is likely to be worth a good sum: and this not because an artificial market for such things has been created, but because of their consummate perfection, their extraordinary unselfconscious beauty and simplicity. There is, in the work of the Shakers, a beauty that is unrivaled because of its genuine spiritual purity—a quality for which there is no adequate explanation, but which can be accounted for in part by the doctrine of the Shakers themselves and their monastic view of manual work as an essential part of the Christian life.

Like the earliest monastic documents, they spoke of the "work of God" which they were called upon to do: the work of building God's "Millennial Church." (In pre-Benedictine documents, the *opus Dei* is not just the liturgy but the whole life of monastic conversion and transformation in Christ.) "God," said one of the Shaker Elders, "is the great Artist and Master Builder; the Gospel is the means; the Ministration are his Laborers, and instruments under his direction. We must labor in union with them to cast all rubbish out of and from around the building, and to labor to bring everything both outward and inward, more and more into order."

This allegorization of Shaker spirituality in terms of "work" represents, of course, no mere abstract fantasy. The Shakers were meticulous workers, with a passion for order, cleanliness, simplicity, practicality, and economy of means. In their "Millennial Laws" they decreed that "Believers may not, in any case, manufacture for sale any article or articles which are superfluously wrought, and which would tend to feed the pride and vanity of man," and "Buildings, mouldings and cornices which are merely for fancy may not be made by Believers." Not only were mirrors, silver spoons, gold and silver watches, and silver pencils banned from the communes as "superfluous," but also "silver tooth picks, three bladed knives, superfluous whips, gay silk handkerchiefs, checkered handkerchiefs made by the world, superfluous suspenders of any kind, and flowery painted clocks." Speaking of a frivolous and "showy" taste for ornament, an Elder said: "The divine man has no right to waste money upon what you would call beauty in his house or daily life, while there are people living in misery." The words unconsciously echo a famous passage in St. Bernard's *Apologia* for Cistercian austerity against Cluny. Yet the Shakers, like the first Cistercians, while giving no conscious thought to the *beauty* of their work, sought only to build honest buildings and to make honest and sturdy pieces of furniture. In doing so, they produced buildings and furniture of extraordinary, unforgettable beauty. True, this beauty has not always been obvious to everyone. Dickens thought Shaker furniture looked "grim," and the spiritual loveliness of Shaker simplicity is not evident to the eye that has submitted passively to the perversion of form by commerce (for example, the absurdities of American automobile design in the fifties).

The mind of the Shaker was directed not merely to the good of the work, the *bonum operis,* or to the advantage of the worker, the *bonum operantis,* but to something that transcended and included both: a kind of wholeness and order and worship that filled the whole day and the whole life of the working community. "Put your hands to work and your hearts to God," said Mother Ann, and again, "Clean your room well, for good spirits will not live where there is dirt. There is no dirt in heaven." The Shakers worked well because their work was a worship offered to God in the sight of his angels—a Biblical phrase which sets the tone for the life of the monks according to the Benedictine Rule. As a matter of fact, the early Shakers expressed a belief that their furniture designs and other patterns had been given to them by the angels and that they manifested heavenly forms, not belonging to the world of fallen men. In point of fact, as E. D. Andrews shows, the Shaker designs were derived from early American colonial patterns which were purified and perfected by the zeal of the Shakers for "primitive rectitude" and their "religious care."

In this perfect fusion of temporal and eternal values, of spirit and matter, the Shakers were in all truth living according to a kind of inspired eschatology in which ambition, personal gain, and even quick material results were not considered important. Of course, whatever was made was made for *use,* and consequently the quality of the work was paramount. What was to be used, was made for "the Church," and in order to share the fruits of labor with the poor and the hungry. The workman had to apply himself to his task with all skill and also with the necessary virtues of humility, patience, and love, contributing thereby to the peace and order of the common life, and "supporting the structure of fraternity."

In no case was work to be done in a hurry or under pressure, or indeed under any form of spiritual compulsion. The competitive spirit was banned because of its occult relationship with lust and violence. Overworking was frowned upon. The workers were encouraged to engage in a variety of tasks, to escape obsession and attachment. At all times their work had to be carried on at a steady, peaceful rhythm, for, as one of the Elders said: "We are not called to labor to excel, or to be like the world; but to excel them in order, union, peace and in good works—works that are truly virtuous and useful to man in this life." He also said: "All work done or things made in the Church for their own use ought to be faithfully and well done, but plain and without superfluity. All things ought to be made according to their order and use." Therefore, as E. D. Andrews says, "an atmosphere of settledness and repose pervaded the [Shaker] villages, as though they were part of the land itself."

Shoddy and hasty workmanship was condemned as "worldly" and unworthy of those living the divine life. Once, when someone had a vision to the effect that brass doorknobs were useless and "worldly," a brother spent considerable time removing all the brass knobs and replacing them with wooden ones.

Some of the sayings of Mother Ann, and other "Shaker sermonettes," give us more light on this attitude of mind, which consisted fundamentally in a devotion to *truth*. A thing or a person is perfect insofar as it is what it is meant to be. Absolute flawlessness is impossible, and the Shakers had no unrealistic dreams about utter perfection. But they were very realistic in striving to make things as they ought to be made so that they served their purpose well. They strove in all things for truth, and made a point of simply *being themselves*. "Do be natural," one of these maxims tells us, "a poor diamond is better than an imitation." "Do not be troubled because you have no great virtues. God made a million spears of grass where He made one tree." "Do be truthful; do avoid exaggeration; if you mean a mile, say a mile, and if you mean one, say one, and not a dozen." "Whatever is really useful is virtuous though it does not at first seem so." Sometimes the simple Shaker maxims remind one of William Blake. This one, for instance: "Order is the creation of beauty. It is heaven's first law, and the protection of souls." Or especially this other: *"Every force evolves a form."*

When we ponder these statements, we discover that they are full of wisdom. They bear witness to a soundness of judgment and a sanity of vision that help to account for the wonders of Shaker craftsmanship: underlying it all is a quasi-mystical sense of *being* and of *reality* crystallized in this simple maxim, which, for all its technical imprecision, reflects something of the great religious philosophies of all time: *"Sincerity is the property of the universe."*

The Shakers came to Kentucky and established themselves at Pleasant Hill, "the topmost bough upon the tree" and "the cream of Kentucky," in 1806. It was indeed pleasant, rolling farm land, a mile or so from the deep wooded gorge of the Kentucky River. The community consisted of recruits from New York, New Jersey, Pennsylvania, and Virginia. Later members came from Europe, including a large colony of Swedes, who were settled in the West Lot House. In the early days, after surviving the usual persecutions, they built a flourishing little town with workshops rising all around the three main "Families" and the Meeting House. John Dunlavy, one of the first Chief Ministers of Pleasant Hill, is said by E. D. Andrews to have had "a clearer insight into religious communism than any other Shaker writer." He wrote of the "united inheritance" and common life of the Shakers, and explicitly compared it with Catholic monasticism. He viewed the monks with a certain approval for "professing greater sanctity than the Church in general" and for their freedom from marital ties. However, he felt that their dependence on vow instead of "conscience alone" was a weakness, and their reliance on alms led them to be "patronized by public approbation and authority," whereas the Shakers were regarded as outcasts. It is almost certain that Dunlavy must have seen something of the first colony of Trappists established, about this time, only fifty miles from Pleasant Hill, in Nelson County. Unlike the persecuted Shakers, the Trappists were surrounded by the approval and concern of the small Catholic colony, and yet they soon left Kentucky, going to Illinois and then returning to France. They returned to Kentucky to build Gethsemani Abbey in 1848.

The Shakers of Pleasant Hill were harassed and plundered by soldiers of both sides in the Civil War (especially before and after the Battle of Perryville, a few miles away, in the fall of 1862). After the war, vocations began to decline, and in the industrial boom of the late nineteenth century the spiritual and social vigor of the Shakers gradually died out. Since they did not marry, there were no children to carry on the community. A few orphans were adopted, but not all of them took to the Shaker life. Twenty years after the Civil War, registrations ceased at Pleasant Hill and the Family Houses began to close.

As the community dwindled, some members left to consolidate with other communities in the east. The Society at Pleasant Hill was officially dissolved in 1910. A few Shakers remained at Pleasant Hill to conduct a small school. The last Shaker of the Pleasant Hill colony, Sister

Mary Settles, a native of Louisville, died there in 1923. For forty years the buildings have been given to other uses or abandoned, but now they are being restored and opened to the public.

After their departure, these innocent people, who had once been so maligned, came to be regretted, loved, and idealized. Too late, the people of Kentucky recognized the extraordinary importance of the spiritual phenomenon that had blossomed out in their midst. Today there is a general awareness that the Shakers made a unique and original contribution to American culture—but it will take more than nostalgia and sentiment to revive their unique combination of "science, religion and inspiration," which remains to us as a mysterious and fascinating "sign" for our times.

NOTES

From Pilgrimage to Crusade

1. Mircea Eliade: *Myths, Dreams and Mysteries* (London, 1960), pp. 59–72. See also, by the same author, *The Myth of the Eternal Return.*
2. *Le Pèlerinage d'Ethérie,* Latin text and French trans. by Hélène Petré (Paris, Sources Chrétiennes, 1948).
3. *La Vie de Moïse,* Greek text and French trans. by Jean Daniélou, 2nd edition (Paris, Sources Chrétiennes, 1955).
4. Valerius of Vierzo: *Epistola de B. Echeria,* P.L. 87:424. See also the important article by Dom Jean Leclercq: "Monachisme et pérégrination du 9ᵉ au 12ᵉ siècles," *Studia Monastica,* Vol. 3, fas. 1 (1961), pp. 33–52. This study traces the development from *stabilitas in peregrinatione* to *peregrinatio in stabilite.*
5. For example, St. Silvinus, St. Ulric, etc., wished to venerate Christ in the very place where He

had accomplished the mysteries of salvation. Leclercq, op. cit., pp. 37–9, 43.

6. H. Von Campenhausen: *Die Asketische Heimatlösigkeit* (Tübingen, 1930). Dom L. Gougaud: *Christianity in Celtic Lands* (London, 1932), pp. 129 ff. N. K. Chadwick: *The Age of Saints in the Early Celtic Church* (London, 1961). Professor Chadwick calls this "one of the most important features of Irish asceticism and its chief legacy to after ages," p. 82.

7. *Adomnan's Life of Columba,* ed., with translation and notes, by the late Alan Orr Anderson and by Marjorie Ogilvie Anderson (Edinburgh, 1961), "de Scotia (Ireland) ad Britanniam *pro Christo peregrinari volens* enavigavit," p. 186.

8. *Navigatio Sancti Brendani abbatis,* ed. by Carl Selmer (Notre Dame, Univ. Publication in Medieval Studies, 1959).

9. See quotations from the Icelandic *Landnámbók* (eleventh or twelfth century) in *Christianity in Celtic Lands,* p. 132. Also a quote from *De Mensura Orbis* by Dicuil (ninth century) in L. Bieler: *Ireland the Harbinger of the Middle Ages* (London, 1963), p. 119.

10. Leclercq, op. cit., pp. 34, 36.

11. Quoted in Chadwick, op. cit., p. 83. Cf.

Leclercq, op. cit., p. 36. See also Leclercq: "La Séparation du monde dans le monachisme du moyen âge" in *La Séparation du Monde: Problèmes de la religieuse de d'aujourd'hui* (Paris 1961), p. 77.

12. Leclercq: "Monachisme et pérégrination," passim., esp. pp. 37, 39, 41.

13. Mircea Eliade: *Myths, Dreams and Mysteries*. Cf. Anselm Stolz, O.S.B.: *Théologie de la Mystique* (Chevetogne); Dom G-M Colombas, O.S.B.: *Paraíso y vida angélica* (Monserrate, 1958).

14. Chadwick: op. cit., pp. 82–3. Kathleen Hughes: "The Irish Monks and Learning," *Los monjes y los estudios* (Poblet, 1963), pp. 66 ff. Eleanor Shipley Duckett: *The Wandering Saints of the Early Middle Ages* (New York 1959), pp. 24–5.

15. Adomnan: op. cit., I.6., "(Cormac) tribus vicibus herimum in ociano laboriose quaesivit . . ." pp. 222–4.

16. Bieler: op. cit., p. 119.

17. *Navigatio Brendani*, c. 11. pp. 22 ff.

18. Dom H. Leclercq, O.S.B.: "Celle," D.A.C.L., ii, 2870, and "Reclus," D.A.C.L., xiv, 2149 ff. Rotha Mary Clay: *The Hermits and Anchorites of England* (London, 1914). P. McNulty and B. Hamilton: "Orientale Lumen et Magistra Latinitas — Greek Influences on Western Mo-

nasticism (900–1100)," *Le Millénaire du Mont Athos* (Chevetogne, 1963), esp. pp. 197–9, 216. Gougaud: *Ermites et Reclus* (Ligugé, 1928).

19. O. Doerr: *Das Institut der Inclusen in Suddeutschland* (Münster, 1934).

20. Chadwick: op. cit., pp. 36, 37, 50–3.

21. See H. Leclercq: "Pèlerinages à Rome," D.A.C.L., xiv, 53–4. This applies more to Franks than to Celts, who were less enthusiastic about pilgrimages to Rome. Witness this ancient verse: "To go to Rome is great labor. The King you seek you will not find unless you bring Him with you." However, St. Moluca, disciple of St. Maedoc, pleaded with his master for permission to go to Rome: *Nisi videro Romam cito moriar.*

22. J. Leclercq: "Monachisme et pérégrination," pp. 42–3.

23. See M-L Soejstedt: *Dieux et héros des celtes,* quoted in R-Y Creston: *Journal de Bord de Saint Brendan* (Paris, 1957), p. 221.

24. See Kenneth Jackson: *A Celtic Miscellany* (Cambridge, Mass., 1951), pp. 301 ff. G. Murphy: *Early Irish Lyrics* (Oxford, 1956). Bieler: op. cit., p. 57.

25. Aussi la pérégrination continue-t-elle a être

présentée comme un forme d'érémitisme, et,
comme telle, dans la logique de la vie monastique. "Monachisme et pérégrination," p. 41.

26. L. Vogel: "Le Pèlerinage pénitentiel," *Revue des
Sc. Rel.,* XXXVIII, 2, 1964, pp. 113 ff. Posch-
mann: *Penance and the Anointing of the Sick* (New
York, 1964). Chadwick: op. cit., p. 103.

27. Chadwick notes that the Scilly Isles had been a
penal settlement in Roman times and that some
Priscillianist heretics had been sent there. She
also cites the questionable tradition of St. Columba's exile for a sin of violence (op. cit.,
p. 102). Vogel (op. cit., p. 127) does not think
the medieval penitential practice of exile is
traceable to Roman law.

28. Council of Seligenstadt, 1022/23. Vogel: op. cit.,
pp. 143–4.

29. Vogel: op. cit., p. 118.

30. Numerous references given in Vogel, pp. 130–1.

31. *Canones sub Edgaro Rege,* England, tenth century, quoted by Vogel, p. 127.

32. St. Gregory of Tours: *Hist. Franc.,* VI, 6.
H. Leclercq: "Pèlerinages à Rome," D.A.C.L.,
xiv, p. 52.

33. D.A.C.L. One penitent even carried an identi-

fication in Latin verse by Venantius Fortunatus, id. 52, on *litterae tractoriae*. See Vogel, p. 133.

34. D.A.C.L., xiv., p. 60.

35. See penitential of Vinnian, n.23, quoted in Bieler, p. 52. Chadwick, p. 102.

36. Le Pèlerinage pénitential aboutit en fait à sélectionner les pires criminels et à les lancer sur les chemins. Vogel, p. 130.

37. Ep. 289.

38. See the famous letter of St. Boniface to Cuthbert of Canterbury (MGH. Epp. III, 78, p. 354), of which Vogel says that it "constitutes a sociological document of the highest order" (op. cit., p. 140).

39. Rule of St. Benedict, C. 38, cf. the quotation of I Cor. 5:5 in the Rule, C. 25.

40. Vogel, p. 126.

41. St. Peter Damian: Opusc. XII., 9–14, 20–25. PL 145:260 ff. G. Peno: "Il Capitulo de Generibus Monachorum nella Traditione Medievale," *Studia Monastica*, 1961, 41 f. J. Leclercq: "Le Poème de Payen Belotin contre les faux ermites," *Rev. Ben.*, 1958, pp. 52 ff.

42. Vogel, p. 145.

43. Ibid., p. 146. Cf. PL 140, 952.

44. Vogel, p. 135.

45. For a complete list of places of pilgrimage, see Vogel, p. 135.

46. *Hagiologium Cistercianse,* Aug. 1.

47. Texts quoted by J. Leclercq: "Monachisme et pérégrination," pp. 40–9.

48. On ne peut s'empêcher de penser que de tels récits étaient, en quelque sorte, les romans d'aventures des moines du moyen âge. J. Leclercq: "Monachisme et pérégrination," p. 40.

49. J. Leclercq, in Leclercq, Vandenbroucke, Bouyer: *Histoire de la Spiritualité Chrétienne,* Vol. II, p. 165.

50. Pilgrims, being foreigners, were naturally suspect, but Moslems usually understood the idea of pilgrimage, which plays a central part in the religion of Islam. St. Willibald was arrested in Edessa in 723 but released when an aged Moslem assured the police that he had many times seen Christians like this one "fulfilling their law." H. Leclercq: D.A.C.L., xiv, p. 163.

51. Vogel, pp. 128–9.

52. Ibid., p. 129, see references.

53. Mourret-Thompson: *History of the Catholic Church* (St. Louis, 1941), Vol. IV, p. 282.

54. J. Leclercq: *Histoire de la Spiritualité Chrétienne,*

Vol. II, p. 166. See references to Dupront, Rousset, etc.

55. Ibid., p. 167.

56. St. Bernard: Letter 458 and *De Laude Novae Militiae.*

57. Mourret-Thompson: op. cit., p. 283.

58. Ch. E. Delaruelle: "L'Idée de croisade chez S. Bernard," *Mélanges S. Bernard* (Dijon, 1953), p. 57.

59. St. Bernard: Letter 363. Cf. Bruno James: *Letters of St. Bernard* (Chicago, 1953).

60. Delaruelle: op. cit., p. 58.

61. Oderic Vital: *Historia Ecclesiastica,* ix, PL 188:652.

62. Delaruelle, p. 54.

63. Delaruelle, p. 66.

64. C. Selmer: "The Vernacular Translations of the *Navigatio Brendani,*" *Medieval Studies,* xvii, 1956, p. 150.

65. H. B. Workman: *Evolution of the Monastic Ideal,* reprint (Boston, 1962), p. 196n.

66. *De Imagine Mundi,* I., 36, PL 172:132.

67. W. H. Babcock: "St. Brendan's Explorations and Islands," *Geographical Review,* July, 1919, pp. 37–46.

68. *The Book of the Foundations,* in the *Complete*

Works of St. Theresa, translated by E. Allison
Peers (New York, 1946), Vol. III.

69. Jean-Paul Sartre: *No Exit.* This expression sums
up the existentialist's meditation on hell.

70. G. Basetti-Sani, O.F.M.: *Mohammed et Saint
François* (Ottawa, 1959).

Virginity and Humanism in the
Western Fathers

1. E. R. Curtius: *European Literature and the Latin
Middle Ages* (New York, 1961), Bollingen Series,
XXV, p. 315.

2. Epistola XXII, *Ad Eustochium,* n. 30, PL 22, col.
416 (vide infra.).

3. Illustrior portio gregis Christi. St. Cyprian: *De
Habitu Virginum,* c. 1. PL 4, col. 440.

4. Op. cit., c. 1, PL 4, col. 440.

5. Clarificemus et portemus Deum in puro et
mundo corpore. Idem., 442.

6. St. Jerome: Epistola XXII, *Ad Eustochium,* n. 38,
PL 22, col. 422. Also: Vidi viros corrumpentes
virgines in doctrinis haereticis et vanam
facientes virginitatem earum. A. Wilmart: "Les
Versions Latines des Sentences d'Evagre," *Revue
Bénédictine,* XXVIII, 1911, pp. 148–51.

7. St. Jerome points out that Christ is not a proud and arrogant Spouse, in implied contrast to men of this world. Epistola XXII, n. 1, PL 22, col. 395. Cf. same letter, n. 2, and n. 18 (col. 405) for allusions to the sufferings of married life, but he goes on to point out that virginal life is also a constant struggle.

8. Estote tales quales vos Deus artifex fecit, estote tales quales vos manus Patris instituit: maneat in vobis facies incorrupta, cervix pura, forma sincera. Op. cit., XXI, col. 459.

9. Servate, Virgines, servate quod esse coepistis, servate quod eritis. . . . Quod futuri sumus jam vos esse coepistis. Vos resurrectionis gloriam in isto saeculo jam tenetis. Op. cit., XXII, col. 462.

10. St. Ambrose: *De Institutione Virginis*, c. 17. Migne, PL 16, col. 331.

11. St. Jerome: Epistola XXII, *Ad Eustochium*, n. 20, PL 22, col. 406.

12. Libertate opus est et audacia. Quae sic in pace metuis, quid faceres in martyrio perpetiendo. St. Jerome: Epist. 130, *Ad Demetriadem*, n. 5, PL 22, col. 1109. Aula regalis est virgo quae non est viro subdita sed Deo soli. St. Ambrose: *De Institutione Virginis*, c. 12, PL 16, col. 324.

13. Stridor Punicae linguae procacia tibi Fescennina

cantabit? Op. cit., 1109. This phrase is reminiscent of Catullus, 61:126: Procax fescennina locutio. "Fescenninan songs" were ribald extemporaneous verses sung by the guests at wedding feasts, made doubly offensive, Jerome suggests, by the harsh Punic accent of Roman Africa.

14. Solent miseri parentes et non plenae fidei Christiano, deformes et aliquo membro debiles filias, quia dignos generos non inveniunt, virginitati tradere. Op. cit., n. 6, col. 1111.

15. Migne, PL 16, col. 305 ff.

16. Ubi ergo tres isti integri, ibi Christus est in medio eorum: qui hos tres intus gubernat et regit ac fideli pace componit. Haec igitur tria integra prae caeteris in se virgo custodiat. Op. cit., cap. 2, col. 309. This is the classical tripartite division of man into *anima* (psyche), *animus* (nous), and *spiritus* (pneuma). Cf. William of St. Thierry: Epistola ad Fratres de Monte Dei, Lib. I, cap. V, PL 184, col. 315 ff.

17. Advertimus itaque per mulierem caeleste illud impletum esse mysterium Ecclesiae, in ea gratia figuratam, propter quam Christus descendit, et aeternum illud opus humanae redemptionis absolvit. Unde et Adam vocavit nomen mulieris suae Vitam; nam et in populis per mulierem

successionis humanae series et propago diffunditur, et per Ecclesiam vita confertur aeterna. Op. cit., cap. 3, col. 311.

18. Mulier excusationem habet in peccato, vir non habet . . . Culpa tua illam absolvit. Ibid., cap. 4, col. 311.

19. Pro te mulier doloribus suis militat et remunerationem ex pena invenit ut per filios per quos affligitur, liberetur. Facta est itaque gratia ex injuria, salus ex infirmitate. Cum salute itaque parit quos in tristitia parturivit. Ibid., col. 312.

20. Non est vitium mulieris esse quod nascitur, sed vitium viri est quaerere in uxore quo saepe tentatur. Ibid.

21. Non possumus reprehendere divini artificis opus sed quem delectat corporis pulchritudo, multo magis illa delectet venustas quae ad imaginem Dei est intus non foris comptior. Ibid., col. 312.

22. Quotidie mulieres jejunant . . . peccatum agnoscunt, accersunt remedium . . . Semel de interdicto mulier manducavit et quotidie jejunio solvit. Qui secutus es errantem, sequere corrigentem. Ibid., col. 313.

23. Ibid., c. 9, col. 320, 321. For *Ordo caritatis,* see

St. Augustine: *De Doctrina Christiana,* Bk. i, cap. 27, PL 34, col. 29.

24. See St. Augustine: *De Doctrina Christiana,* especially Bk. ii., PL 16, col. 36 ff. Cassian: *Conlatio* XIV, "De Spirituali Scientia," PL 49:953 ff.

25. Porta clausa es virgo, nemo aperiat januam tuam quam semel clausit Sanctus et Verus qui habet clavem David qui aperit et nemo claudit, claudit et nemo aperit: APERUIT TIBI SCRIPTURAS, NEMO EAS CLAUDAT: CLAUSIT PUDOREM TUUM NEMO APERIAT EUM. St. Ambrose, op. cit., c. 9, col. 321.

26. Cf. John Cassian: *Conlatio* I, cc. 4–8, PL 49:485 ff.

27. Habeto ergo tecum hunc ignem in pectore tuo qui te resuscitet, ne frigus tibi perpetuae mortis irrepat. St. Ambrose: op. cit., c. 11, col. 323.

28. Semel mundo mortua ne quaeso tetigeris ne attiminaveris quae sunt istius saeculi: sed semper in psalmis et hymnis et canticis spiritualibus abducas te ab hujus saeculi conversatione non homini sed Deo cantans. Et sicut sancta faciebat Maria, conferas in corde tuo. Quasi bona quoque agnicula rumines in ore tuo praecepta divina. Ibid., cap. 16, col. 330.

29. Cibis praeferto doctrinam. St. Jerome: Epist. 22, n. 24, PL 22, col. 409.

30. Ibid.

31. Ibid., n. 17, col. 404.

32. *Speculum Charitatis.*

33. Tenenti codicem somnus obrepat, et cadentem faciem pagina sancta suscipiat. St. Jerome: op. cit., n. 17, col. 404.

34. Op. cit., n. 29, col. 416.

35. Ibid., n. 30, col. 416.

36. Epistola XXVII, *Ad Marcellam,* PL 22, col. 431, 432. Someone counted the number of classical quotations in Jerome's letters before and after this vision. They are most numerous in his later letters. See E. K. Rand: *Founders of the Middle Ages* (Cambridge, 1928).

37. Unde est tibi providendum ne ineptiis blanditiis feminarum, dimidiata dicere verba filia consuescat, et in auro atque purpura ludere: quorum alterum linguam, alterum moribus officit: ne discat in tenero quod ei postea dediscendum est. Epistola CVII, *Ad Laetam,* n. 4, PL 22, col. 872.

38. Ibid., col. 871.

39. Ibid.

40. Ibid.

41. Ibid., n. 9, col. 874.

42. Ibid.

43. Ibid., n. 11, col. 875.

44. Oratio lectioni, lectio orationi succedat. Ibid., col. 875.

45. Ibid.

46. Pro gemmis et serico divinos codices amet. Ibid., n. 12, col. 875.

47. Discat primo Psalterium et in Proverbiis Salomonis erudiatur ad vitam . . . In Ecclesiaste consuescat quae sunt mundi calcare . . . in Job virtutis et patientiae exempla sectetur . . . Ad Evangelia transeat numquam ea positura de manibus . . . Apostolorum Acta et Epistola tota cordis imbibat voluntate. Cumque pectoris sui cellaria his opibus locupletaverit, mandet memoriae Prophetas, etc. . . . Ibid., n. 12, col. 876.

48. Ad ultimum sine periculo discat Cantica Canticorum. Ibid. Jerome adds that she must "beware of all the Apocrypha." Patristic studies are not to be neglected either: she must concentrate especially on St. Cyprian (Cypriani opuscula semper in manu teneat), Athanasius, and Hilary. St. Jerome is once again most concerned for the purity of virginal faith, which must conform perfectly to the mind of the virginal

Church, thus reproducing in the world the faith of the Mother of God.

49. Virum bonum dicendi peritum a prima aetate suscipiens, per cunctas artes ac disciplinas nobilium litterarum erudiendum esse monastravit, quem merito ad defendendum totius civitatis vota requirerent. Cassiodorus: *Instituta,* II, ii, n. 10; Mynors, p. 104.

50. Ut in omnibus sensibus et operibus ejus Christus eluceat, Christum intendat, Christus loquatur. *De Institutione Virginis,* c. 17, col. 333.

51. Cum avum viderit in pectus ejus transiliat, collo dependeat, nolenti Alleluia decantet. Epistola 107, n. 4, col. 872.

The English Mystics

1. David Knowles: *The English Mystical Tradition* (New York, 1961).

2. Hugh Farmer: *The Monk of Farne* (Baltimore, 1961).

3. *The Medieval Mystics of England,* ed. with an introduction by Eric Colledge (New York, 1961).

4. *Un Educateur monastique: Aelred de Rievaulx* (Paris, 1959).

5. Thomas Traherne: *Centuries of Meditations* (New York, 1961).

6. Ibid., Introduction, p. xvi.

7. Ibid., p. 94.

8. Ibid., p. 91.

9. I am indebted to Etta Gullick for permission to quote from her unpublished manuscript of the seventeenth-century English text of Benet's *Rule of Perfection.*

10. *The Scale of Perfection,* in modern English by Dom Gerard Sitwell, O.S.B. (London, 1953), p. 83. See also Dom G. Sitwell: "Walter Hilton," *English Spiritual Writers,* ed. by C. Davis (New York, 1961).

11. *The Cloud of Unknowing,* translated and with introductory commentary by Ira Progoff (New York, 1957).

12. Ibid., p. 61.

13. See P. Molinari: *Julian of Norwich, the Teaching of a 14th Century English Mystic* (New York, 1958).

14. *Revelations of Divine Love,* in a new translation by James Walsh, S.J. (London, 1961).

15. Ibid., p. 53.

16. Ibid.

17. Ibid., p. 83.

18. In *Poets and Mystics* (London, 1953).

19. C. Pepler: "Richard Rolle," *English Spiritual Writers,* ed. by C. Davis (New York, 1961). Cf. Pepler: *The English Religious Heritage* (London, 1958).

Russian Mystics

1. See Igor Smolitsch: "Le Mont Athos et la Russie," in *Le Millénaire du Mont Athos* (Chevetogne, Belgium, 1963), p. 299. Smolitsch calls this opinion of Leontiev's a "somewhat unusual estimate."

Protestant Monasticism

1. François Biot: *The Rise of Protestant Monasticism* (Helicon, 1964), 161 pp.

Pleasant Hill

1. These pages rely heavily on material collected and published by Edward Deming Andrews, especially in his books *Shaker Furniture* and *The People Called Shakers.* The latter (New York, Ox-

ford University Press, 1953) is the best introduction to Shaker history and thought. It is now being reissued in a new edition by the Indiana University Press.

Ex parte ordinis

Nihil obstat
Fr. M. Benjamin Clark, O.C.S.O.
Fr. M. Shane Regan, O.C.S.O.

Imprimi potest
Fr. M. Ignace Gillet, O.C.S.O.
Abbot General, Rome, September 9, 1965

Nihil obstat
Edward J. Montano, S.T.D.

Imprimatur
Terence J. Cooke, D.D.
Vicar General, Archdiocese of New York
January 24, 1967

LIBRARY OF CONGRESS
CATALOGING-IN-PUBLICATION DATA

Merton, Thomas, 1915–1968.
Ways of the Christian mystics/Thomas Merton.
p.   cm. — (Shambhala pocket classics)
ISBN 1-57062-030-X
1. Mysticism—History.   I. Title.   II. Series.
BV5075.M47   1994   94-8330
248.2′2′09—dc20   CIP

(*Continued on next page*)

ZEN AND THE BIRDS OF APPETITE
by Thomas Merton

ZEN LESSONS: The Art of Leadership
Translated by Thomas Cleary

THE ZEN TEACHING OF HUANG PO
Translated by John Blofeld